Acknowledgements

D0299355

I would like to thank Richard Berthoud for getting me involved in this project and for his advice and comments from its earliest stages. I am grateful to all those who read and commented on drafts of this book for their valuable observations and corrections: Martin Barnes, Richard Berthoud, David Colclough, Gary Craig and Stephen Jenkins all provided detailed and constructive criticism. It is undoubtedly a very different – and better – book for their contributions. I, however, take full responsibility for any inaccuracies or infelicities that remain. I am very grateful to Alison Key for encouraging this book into existence and for seeing it through to publication. I would also like to thank my colleagues and students at the Department of Sociology, University of Essex for providing me with the stimulating and congenial environment within which this book was produced.

I am grateful to the Department for Work and Pensions Analytical Services Division for access to the data of Households Below Average Income 1999/00. They, however, bear no responsibility for my further analysis of the data.

About the author

Lucinda Platt is lecturer in sociology at the University of Essex, where she is responsible for teaching on British and comparative social policy. Her current research interests are child poverty, ethnic minorities and welfare state history. She has published in the areas of ethnic minority disadvantage, the health of young people, social security and child poverty. Before moving into research, she was a community worker and an adult literacy teacher.

Poverty among
ethnic minority groups
in Britain

Parallel
lives?

Lucinda Platt

CPAG • 94 White Lion Street • London N1 9PF

CPAG promotes action for the relief, directly or indirectly, of poverty among children and families with children. We work to ensure that those on low incomes get their full entitlements to welfare benefits. In our campaigning and information work we seek to improve benefits and policies for low-income families in order to eradicate the injustice of poverty. If you are not already supporting us, please consider making a donation, or ask for details of our membership schemes and publications.

© Poverty Publication 107

Published by CPAG
94 White Lion Street, London N1 9PF

© CPAG 2002

ISBN 1 901698 49 1

A CIP record for this book is available from the British Library

Cover and design by Devious Designs 0114 2755634
Typeset by Boldface 020 7253 2014
Printed by Russell Press 0115 9784505

Contents

Contents

Foreword

Thanks to the welcome decline in the tendency to divide Britain into white and non-white communities and to homogenise them, we are beginning to appreciate their internal differences and the damages of misleading generalisations. Contrary to general belief, not all Asians are high achievers economically and educationally. The Chinese and East African Asians are, but Pakistanis, Bangladeshis and Afro-Caribbeans are not, and Indians hover in the middle. Even the high-achieving groups contain pockets of poverty, just as the low-achieving ones include some who have done quite well. The incidence of poverty is certainly higher in ethnic minority groups than in the country at large, but not uniformly so.

The increasing appreciation of diversity within the ethnic minority communities calls for a radical revision of the traditional approach to the subject. We need new methodological and conceptual tools to reach out to and uncover the differential achievements and failures of different clusters of individuals in different ethnic groups. We also need a sophisticated and nuanced explanatory framework that cuts across the usual structuralist versus culturalist debate. Human beings are inevitably conditioned by the constraints and possibilities of their place in the wider economic and social structure. However, they are also creative beings, who draw upon their cultural resources, social networks, historical experiences, and powers of imagination to exploit their opportunities and overcome the obstacles. Structures are not passively given, but subject to human mediation. And human creativity is not limitless but operates within the framework of objective constraints.

Parallel Lives? represents a major contribution to the subject of ethnicity and poverty. Using sophisticated tools to define poverty, disadvantage and ethnicity and mobilising all available data, it skilfully explores which ethnic groups suffer from what degree and kind of relative deprivation and disadvantage. It then goes on to explain the reasons for this, and highlights the complex interplay of structural, social and cultural factors. As it rightly argues, ethnicity, class, gender, generation, education, area of residence, etc are all important factors, each mediating and being in turn mediated by others. This is why some ethnic groups, but not others, make a successful transition from the declining traditional sectors of industry to the high skill and service-based economy, or move from the

New Deal for the Long-Term Unemployed to full-time unsubsidised employment. Such a nuanced explanation has important policy implications, and requires, among other things, a reconsideration of the highly popular, but flawed, area-based approach. The Runnymede Report on the *Future of Multi-Ethnic Britain* dealt with many of these issues. The present work corrects, updates, builds on, and in some cases goes beyond, its conclusions. I found it a most reliable guide to this complex area, and hope that others will learn as much from it as I have.

Lord Bhikhu Parekh
Professor Global Governance,
London School of Economics

One
Introduction

In Britain today the chances of poverty vary enormously according to ethnicity. For example, at the turn of the millennium nearly three-quarters of Bangladeshi children were living in families in the bottom fifth of the income distribution compared to a quarter of white children.[1] At a time of growing interest in issues of social cohesion and political emphasis on an 'inclusive society', what are the prospects for ethnic minority groups of full participation? To what extent are they relegated to a limited existence through lower standards of living? What is being done about it? And what are the prospects for the future? These are the questions that this book attempts to address. It therefore provides a resource for the 'facts' of ethnic minority poverty and its various causes, as well as an evaluation of the prospects for the future. It is intended to be relevant to those concerned with the situation of different minority groups, to those with an interest in inequalities in society and to those involved in developing and evaluating policy.

In his report of the investigation into the riots in Bradford, Burnley and Oldham of Summer 2001, Ted Cantle famously referred to groups living 'parallel lives'.[2] He was referring primarily to the consequences of geographical segregation. This book takes up the image of parallel lives to question the extent to which particular minority groups can be said to have an existence that runs in parallel to that of the population as a whole through greater rates of poverty and deprivation. It identifies the ways in which past discrimination and disadvantage has affected the current welfare of minority groups. It evaluates the extent to which the current structures and policies perpetuate or mitigate deprivation in the present. And it reflects on the prospects for the future: for today's children in adulthood, for adults in their later years and for future generations. It considers what attempts have been made to tackle ethnic minority disadvantage and what recommendations have been proposed.

In the early 1990s, the Child Poverty Action Group published *Poverty in Black and White*, a broad synthesis of information relating to different forms of disadvantage experienced by minority ethnic groups.[3] Since then there have been substantial improvements in the availability of data and extent of information on the experience of different minority ethnic groups, accompanied by an increase in research into the specifics and causes of such experience.[4] Powerful local qualitative studies emanating predominantly from the voluntary sector and voluntary sector funding bodies drew attention to issues of disadvantage and discrimination in the 1980s and 1990s. They illuminated the experience of minority groups in relation to housing, to health services, to employment and to social security, highlighting both the persistence of discrimination years after the principal race relations legislation of 1976 and the perpetuation of the disadvantage experienced by the migrant generations within the British-born population.[5] These studies both stimulated and were complemented by increased quantitative sources of information in the 1990s that could reveal the patterns of experience across Britain's main ethnic minority groups as a whole and enable a more definitive understanding of the prevalence of poverty among the different groups. The resulting picture has revealed a complex story: a story of diversity, of continuity and of change.

The recognition of the wide diversity of experience across minority groups challenged monolithic understandings of the operation of racism within society, leading to greater attention to the complexity of processes of discrimination, their relationship to outcomes, and to the ways in which different 'racisms' structure the lives of members of minority ethnic groups.[6] The increasing awareness of wide diversity of experience between minority groups, which began to replace a 'white'-'non-white' dichotomy, also led to an acceptance that the same explanatory framework could not adequately account for the outcomes of different ethnic groups. Instead, the particular constellation of influences and pressures was relevant to how they translated into group welfare or lack of welfare: into relative advantage or relative disadvantage. Research also highlighted the importance of taking account of social class background in constructing explanations. The constraints that operate on the basis of the social class that someone is born into interact with the constraints of ethnicity and the way it is regarded and treated. The result is that ethnicity has different effects across classes; and, at the same time, class is more or less salient for the outcomes of different ethnic groups. Research that revealed continuities across 'first' and 'second' generation minority group members – that is, across the migrant generation and those born in Britain – similarly complicated accounts that were based on assumptions about the processes of migration. At the same time, observation of the successes of the Chinese and Indian minority groups in education and employment served to counter to a certain degree the pessimistic and essentialist attitudes sometimes engendered by evidence of entrenched and enduring disadvantage elsewhere. Success and achievement, even against the odds, were clearly possible – raising the crucial question of what made them possible. What circumstances enable minority ethnic groups to flourish is a question to which any discussion of ethnic minority poverty would hope to contribute.

The 1990s have also seen developments at policy level. Wider recognition of disadvantage and ongoing discrimination have both fuelled and been sustained by the greater availability of reliable national data on the ethnic minority populations that took off with the inclusion of an ethnic group question in the 1991 Census. Concern has been shown about entrenched and enduring disadvantage, about limited opportunities and about the failure of certain sections of the British population to realise their potential – concerns which map closely with the Labour Government's 'inclusive' agenda, which it asserted on coming to power in 1997. But these concerns have also been matched by fears and anxieties about the consequences of the failure sufficiently to address racist and dislocated aspects of society. Such anxieties came to the fore in response to the murder of Stephen Lawrence and the subsequent enquiry, and to the riots that erupted in a number of northern towns in the summer of 2001. The result has been a much greater responsiveness to issues of ethnic minority disadvantage – as seen, for example, in the establishment of a team to look at labour market issues within the Performance and Innovation Unit of the Cabinet Office – alongside the first race relations legislation for over a quarter of a century, in the form of the Race Relations Amendment Act 2000.

This current account of ethnic minority poverty is, therefore, timely. It brings together findings that demonstrate the extreme poverty of certain groups and the excess poverty that characterises the minority group experience as a whole. It comes at a time when research has given us a much more sophisticated understanding of the ways in which minority group members become, and remain, poor, and yet still leaves many issues unclear or unresolved. It also captures a moment when policy in relation to some of the causes and associations of ethnic minority poverty is being developed, but when its impact has yet to be ascertained. It therefore not only synthesises and evaluates the state of knowledge, but also raises questions to which we still lack answers. It considers the direction of current policy and suggests ways by which we might improve or evaluate its effectiveness.

This book deals with ethnic minority poverty in Britain: the extent of poverty among different minority groups and how this compares with the experience of the population as a whole. The most recent evidence reveals the large amount of poverty experienced by different minority groups and the shocking extent of ethnic inequality. There have been increasing attempts to explain how these patterns of poverty have come about: what has created them and what sustains them. The different causal factors associated with ethnic minority poverty, such as discrimination, unemployment, low wages, and disadvantage within the benefits system are discussed, and the research evidence on the different topics is synthesised and evaluated. While the book does not offer any final explanation for the differences in experience, it does consider how far the available accounts take us in understanding them. Explanation often implies its own solutions, and the book also analyses the policy implications of research findings on ethnic minority poverty. It assesses the possibilities for mitigating minority group poverty and considers whether policies appear to be moving in that direction.

The book does not cover issues relating to minority ethnic groups or their experiences that do not have a *direct* bearing on poverty. Suggestions for additional reading in health and housing, where substantial differences can also be observed between ethnic groups are, however, offered in the appendix at the end of the book.

Structure of the book

The structure of the book is, therefore, as follows. Chapter 2 develops the rationale and scope of the book. It covers definitional issues in relation to the classification of ethnic groups and to the measurement of poverty. It also clarifies the meaning of discrimination and the distinction between direct and indirect discrimination enshrined in the 1976 Race Relations Act.

Chapter 3 sets the context for its survey of minority group poverty by indicating levels of poverty in the population as a whole, according to a number of different measures. It then outlines the available information on ethnic minority poverty: its degree and concentration. This chapter, then, constitutes the 'facts' of minority groups' poverty, and forms the heart of the book.

This account of minority groups' poverty implies a number of associated or possibly causal factors, which are picked up on and explored in

Chapters 4 to 6. As these chapters demonstrate, the issues that are associated with higher poverty rates among certain minority groups may themselves require explanation in terms of other factors. For example, much
Pakistani poverty can be associated with high unemployment rates, but
these unemployment rates themselves require consideration in relation to
such factors as educational level, area-based disadvantage and discrimination. The divisions introduced in these chapters are thus, to a certain
extent, artificial, but the different emphases of different explanatory frameworks can be important in implying distinct solutions. For example, an
explanation which focuses on discrimination will suggest the need for
more stringent race relations legislation, while an account which explores
the impact of different qualification levels may, instead, imply that effective
educational policies are the key. Thus, the different areas covered by these
chapters relate to considerations of different forms of actual or potential
policy response.

Chapters 4 to 6 consider two broad forms of explanation of excess
poverty among particular minority groups. Chapter 4 explores those that
are seen as intrinsic to the group, often regarded as 'cultural' explanations. It looks at the role of family structure, of patterns of family formation,
and at levels of economic activity, particularly the wide variations in the
rate of female economic activity.

Poverty is often associated with disadvantage in the labour market:
low pay and unemployment. Chapter 5 outlines the extent of labour market disadvantage and analyses what are often seen as structural causes
affecting ethnic minorities' relative disadvantage in the workplace: occupational sector; areas of geographical concentration coinciding with areas
of de-industrialisation; and different levels of 'human capital' (education). It
reveals the extent to which such explanations are insufficient to explain the
extent of minority group disadvantage and takes up the issue of employment discrimination. The extent to which the distinction between 'ethnically'- and 'structurally'-based explanatory frameworks can be sustained
is also considered.

Chapter 6 considers the experience of poverty of those who are
workless and questions how well the benefits system responds to the
needs of minority groups and the extent to which it may exacerbate
poverty.

A theme running through the explanatory accounts considered in all
three chapters is the role of discrimination, either in establishing the structural constraints that now prevail or in determining how cultural factors are
linked to poverty. While current discrimination may be construed as a

to outcomes tells us, then, not 'simply' about particular forms of disadvantage; it also reflects on the whole of our society, on the justice or lack of justice in which everyone is necessarily implicated.

Although the relative disadvantage of minority groups has long been recognised, it is only since the early 1990s that data sources have become available that make it possible systematically to assess income disadvantage and the associated factors according to ethnic group. Alongside this massive increase in the availability of ethnically coded data has come the recognition of the misleading nature of discussions, which aggregate the experience of minority ethnic groups and compare them as a whole to the white population. The great differences *between* minority groups have begun to be charted and seen as a crucial factor in developing appropriate explanatory frameworks and policy responses. This has also further facilitated criticism of minority-majority comparisons, which tend to normalise the experience of the majority and perceive the minority experience as somehow deviant. The very complexity of poverty patterns and the different weight of different factors for different situations have made it possible to deconstruct such unhelpful dichotomies.

Therefore, despite the persistence of some research which aggregates minority groups, either through statistical needs for larger numbers or as part of a single overarching account, this book avoids treating the minority experience as a whole, contrasted with the 'white' population. Instead, it emphasises the differences in experience that pertain to different groups. Recognition of variation in experience requires different strategies of explanation and invites a more complex account of the situation of groups than a simple stress on racism as the factor 'filling the gap'. This is not to downplay the significance of racism in individuals' lives and on their life chances. There is a danger, though, that recourse to racism as an explanation obscures a rigorous examination of the *processes* by which some people end up poor. This book, therefore, focuses on the discrete patterning of past experience (including past discriminatory processes), present characteristics and the impact of structural factors that result in distinct outcomes for the different groups considered. In fact, one of the advantages of such an approach, which comprehends the complex of factors that result in poverty for individual groups, is that it can enable a clearer understanding of how discrimination affects life chances.

The measurement of poverty also provides a means to evaluate and propose policy measures that attempt to reduce injustice and mitigate disadvantage. It is hoped that the discussion presented here may also have some practical value in terms of thinking through the implications of policy in relation to the causes or potential causes of minority group dis-advantage. While current terminology often stresses 'social exclusion' rather than 'poverty', the impossibility of separating or distinguishing between them is clear from policy statements themselves, as discussed below.[3] This book prefers to use the simpler, but no less contested, term 'poverty' to highlight not only the differential income experience of differ-ent groups, but also how income and life chances are inseparably inter-twined, and to explore the relevance of ethnicity within that mesh.

What follows, then, is a synthesis of the most up-to-date informa-tion on poverty concerning the different minority groups in Britain. It demonstrates comparisons and contrasts between the poverty experi-ence of the minority groups and the factors associated with that poverty. It does this not so much by comparison with a normalised 'white' experi-ence, but by looking at the extent to which patterns in the population as a whole, to which each minority group contributes, are reflected in the individual group's experience. Information on the comparable position of the white group is, nevertheless, also included.

The remainder of this chapter is concerned with issues of definition and clarification. It begins by taking up the concept of discrimination. Given that issues of racism and discrimination are critical to our under-standing of the experience of minority ethnic groups and have an impor-tant role to play in accounting for their experience of poverty, what follows is an outline of how discrimination is defined in law, as well as some of the ways it has been formulated beyond that.

Discrimination

Discrimination can affect ethnic minorities and increase their risk of pover-ty at a number of different stages: it can affect their educational experi-ence with a knock-on effect for qualifications and employment; it can affect their employment chances and what sort of job they get, as well as their pay; it can affect their experience within employment and opportuni-ties for promotion; and it can affect their experience of and success in claiming benefits. For those out of work it can affect how they are treated within the benefits system or the assistance they get with finding work. Current or previous discrimination in housing can cause constraints on what employment is accessible and viable, as well as having a potential impact on physical or psychological well-being, which may in turn affect earnings prospects. Discrimination can also affect the ability to build up assets, which may have implications for the next generation, as well as for the current generation in later life or in times of crisis.

Discrimination can take effect in a number of areas to deny equal opportunity or to limit possibilities for avoiding or escaping poverty. Migrating minority group members were constrained by discrimination in terms of their settlement and employment opportunities at a time when there were no checks on treating people differentially in services or employment according to their ethnic group. These original effects have had some long-lasting consequences, as Chapter 5 illustrates. In addition, despite legislation outlawing discrimination that goes back some 35 years, there is still evidence that discrimination continues to operate to restrict and constrain minority group members, evidence which is covered in subsequent chapters. Increasingly, there is also discussion about how discrimination operates differently in relation to different minority groups. For example, Modood has argued that religion should be seen to be a critical factor when considering discrimination and that it is Muslims who are most subject to racist assumptions and actions.[4]

Racism

Racism is both a *form* of discrimination and encompasses more than the latter term comprehends. Racism is a form of discrimination in that it is an expression of differential treatment or approach that is specifically based on notions of immutable, naturalised difference and the inferiority of those seen as other.[5] Such perceived differences and the stereotypes based on them, which regard individuals as representatives of assumed group characteristics, relate to both physical attributes, such as phenotype, and cultural attributes such as dress, manner, or habits. While it is widely acknowledged that 'races' do not exist, in much discussion it continues to be implied that they do.[6] And the belief in the meaningfulness of 'race' that underlies racism results in behaviours, language and action that can have a profound effect on those subjected to it. Discrimination can encompass behaviours and attitudes that are not overtly or even consciously racist, but through ensuing actions have a differential impact on those from a minority ethnicity. Racism, on the other hand, is more than discrimination insofar as discrimination focuses on outcomes, particularly material and economic outcomes, whereas racism refers to all those words, attitudes and actions that denigrate, exclude, disadvantage or subjugate others.

The *Parekh Report* supplies evidence of both the extent and the nature of the experience of racism, including the following quotation from a member of a focus group:

> 'Last week this happened. I was at the bus stop and this yellow car was just driving past and four white lads just shouted out, 'Paki, we're coming to get you'…All I was doing was I was at that bus stop just doing the same thing as anyone else, just waiting for a bus. There was no need and it just makes you feel gutted.'[7]

The pain and indignities caused by daily encounters with racism are in a sense immeasurable and therefore harder to relate to the discussion of ascertained poverty that makes up this book;[8] the impact of racist assault and damage, while clearly measurable on a number of levels, are beyond the more specific focus on poverty. Nevertheless, the experience of racism can both contribute to exclusion and can have significant effects on quality of life regardless of income. It can contribute to poverty by restricting people's residential choices and their geographical mobility. It can also form an outcome of poverty, both in the sense that it is harder to avoid adverse situations when you are poor, and because racism as an expression of power will more effectively be applied to those who are relatively powerless through poverty.

The two related concepts of discrimination and racism come together in the term 'institutional racism' rendered a critical part of the lexicon by Sir William Macpherson's use of it in his report on the inquiry into the death of Stephen Lawrence.

Racial discrimination in British law

The first Race Relations Act was introduced in 1965, covering access to public amenities such as swimming pools, with a further Race Relations Act in 1968 outlawing discrimination in housing and employment. However, it is from the 1976 Race Relations Act that legislative attempts to combat discrimination have really been counted. The Race Relations Act 1976 was explicitly modelled on the Sex Discrimination Act of the preceding year. The Commission for Racial Equality (which was created from former bodies as part of the Act) has outlined the coverage of the Race Relations Act 1976 as follows:

'The 1976 Act outlaws direct and indirect discrimination and victimisation in certain areas.

Direct discrimination means less favourable treatment on racial grounds. In practice, either it must be obvious that the treatment is on racial grounds, for example racial harassment, or there must be evidence that a person of a different racial group in similar circumstances would not have received the same treatment.

Indirect discrimination is concerned with the imposition of a condition or requirement – not necessarily formally adopted, but customarily operational within an organisation – that does not refer to race, but which in its application operates to the disadvantage of a particular racial group, as members of that group are proportionately less able to comply with the condition or requirement.

Indirect discrimination is unlawful if it cannot be justified on non-racial grounds.

Indirect discrimination can have the effect of barring certain racial groups from desired outcomes, such as admission to a school, or subjecting them to unwanted outcomes, such as selection for redundancy. As caselaw has illustrated, it is often impossible to draw a clear line between direct and indirect discrimination.

Victimisation

This has a special legal meaning in the Race Relations Act. It occurs if you are treated less favourably because you have complained about racial discrimination or supported someone else who has.'[9]

It is unlawful, under the Act, to discriminate against anyone on grounds of 'race', colour, nationality, ethnic or national origin. Caselaw has defined which groups are covered by the Act. There is no definitive list of those so covered. To date, caselaw has defined Jews, Gypsies, Sikhs, Irish and Welsh as covered by the Act, while it has denied that Muslims or Rastafarians are covered.

Yet the introduction of the 1976 Race Relations Act clearly did not put an end to discrimination, direct or indirect, in the workplace or in public services – as the rest of this book makes clear.

Institutional racism

The inadequacy of existing legislation in solving the 'race relations' issue was highlighted with great force by the murder of Stephen Lawrence and the subsequent inquiry into how the murder was investigated.[10] In his report of inquiry, Macpherson attempted to avoid the identification of particular individuals for a problem that he felt was endemic to the whole institution. He tried to capture, with the term 'institutional racism', the ways that professional practice was compromised by ingrained assumptions and stereotyping that were explicitly or implicitly endorsed by the whole organisation, with a failure of leadership to remedy them and a culture which sustained and perpetuated them. Rather than simply apportion blame to individuals for specific failings, he tried to stress the relevance of ignorance and even 'unwitting prejudice' in contributing to those failings. He also extended the concept beyond the police service and indicated a need for all institutions to reflect on their practices and their professionalism and for the need for responsibility for the actions of those at junior level to be taken by those at senior level.

The Government's response to Macpherson's report was the Race Relations Amendment Act of 2000. This, the first piece of race relations legislation since 1976, increased the onus on public sector organisations to *demonstrate* that they were operating in a non-discriminatory fashion. It also strengthened the hand of the Commission for Racial Equality, giving it options for enforcement – rather than simply recommendation – in cases where it had conducted formal investigations. There should now be much greater scope, therefore, for ascertaining both the extent of discrimination and for recourse to standards set within organisations themselves for changing bad practice and implementing approaches which are consciously concerned with greater equality. The relevance of this Act to issues of ethnic minority poverty is discussed further in the concluding chapter to this book.

The next section of this chapter takes up the issue of definition and classification of minority ethnic groups, before considering the meaning of poverty. This is followed by a discussion of different forms of poverty measurement. Highlighted at the end of this section is the fact that child poverty, though not the subject of the book, forms a recurrent theme throughout. I also outline the Government's position on poverty and poverty measurement, before providing a definition of social class – another recurrent theme throughout the book, given the recourse to notions of social class in many recent attempts to account for minority groups' disadvantaged situation. The chapter then goes on to consider sources of available information on the subject of ethnic minority poverty, which are employed in the remainder of the book.

Ethnic group definition and classification

The range of minority ethnic groups considered in this volume is dependent on the sources available and the forms of classification used within those sources. Up to 1991 direct information from survey or administrative data on minority groups was limited and non-standardised in terms of the categories counted and considered – and the ways in which they were classified.[11] Some surveys, for example, used the observation of the surveyor rather than direct information from the respondent to classify groups.[12] In terms of censuses, before 1991 information was collected on place of birth only, which was often used as a proxy for ethnicity in research, but never a fully satisfactory one since some members of the 'majority' or white population would have been born abroad and some minority group members were born in Britain. The 1991 Census, therefore, introduced a self-definition question on ethnic group with a limited number of options (see Table 2.1). Those who felt unable to respond to the available options or wished to clarify an 'other' response could write in their self-definition, on the basis of which they would either be reallocated to one of the other groups or remain in the residual – and ultimately meaningless – classification of 'other'. Increasingly classification systems have tended to conform to that used in the 1991 Census (though often without the write-in option), despite the disquiet expressed by many about the contrasting assumptions enshrined within that system.[13]

The categories used in 1991 were themselves altered for the 2001 Census with the introduction of a set of 'mixed' categories. While the new classification has been welcomed on many fronts,[14] the new 'mixed' categories are problematic for a number of reasons. Firstly, at a purely pragmatic level they prevent comparison over time, as the population estimates supplied in Chapter 4 illustrate. There is no direct translation from one set of categories to the next. More importantly, they do not, I would argue, represent a conceptual improvement on the old set of categories, as they conflate questions of parentage with questions of identity. While it has been widely acknowledged that the 1991 ethnic group question was not really asking about ethnicity or ethnic identity – that was, at least, what it purported to do.[15] While the mixed categories may appeal intuitively to those who felt constrained by the 1991 categories and feel that they more nearly reflect the complexity of identity and affiliation, in fact they tend to confuse the issue of what is being measured and why. If the question was intending to capture those groups which have had distinct experiences both through they way they have been treated – how people respond to their difference or apparent difference – and as a result of their cultural characteristics, then the extent to which those categories continue to, or fail to, distinguish the groups over time is itself important. The pragmatic issue of comparison over time is related to the conceptual issue of what is being measured. Obviously people have multiple and overlapping identities,[16] but the ethnic group question is not dealing with this. Instead it seeks a single point of reference. To imply that certain responses capture a greater complexity of identification is somewhat disingenuous. Issues of family formation and partnership, and the changing configuration of populations are clearly of interest. But this cannot fully be answered by the new ethnic group question as it stands. It may give part of the answer, but will not be informative about those who do not respond to the 'mixed' identifications, but nevertheless have a varied heritage. Both these areas of patterns of partnership and developing identities are ones which merit further attention. Meanwhile, for the purposes of the Census and comparable classifications, it would, I suggest, be more helpful to disentangle the two points of 'parentage' and 'identity' with separate questions. The identity question could then perhaps incorporate the possibility of a hyphenated identity as has been argued for and which also appears to have some broad support.[17] This new 2001 Census classification is gradually being adopted by other sources, such as the *Labour Force Survey*, but currently, published information in many cases continues to operate with the 1991 classifications and aggregated combinations of the groups, as will be seen in the tables in this volume.

But what does 'ethnic group' actually mean? And how does that correspond to the classifications available? How, too, does ethnic group correspond to discussions of race (or the alternative, and preferred, formulation 'race'), which are still common in the literature? In Britain the idiom of race has largely been superseded by that of ethnic groups, with the acknowledgement that to speak of race (at least without the inverted commas) is inappropriate because it implies that 'races' exist as biological entities. An ethnic group is, theoretically, one where the association with both a particular origin and specific customs is adopted by people themselves to establish a shared identity.[18] Ethnic groups are therefore self-conscious and have claimed identities, and include the various 'white' populations of Britain. In practice, however, expressed identity is often not captured (or intended to be captured) in sources of information about minority ethnic groups: questions are not left open and the options offered indicate that in seeking information on ethnic origin, surveys and censuses are attempting to capture something about the 'non-white' population of Britain aggregated to reflect a number of common aspects of 'identity' such as immigration history, forbears' nationality, region of origin, religion etc. The unspoken assumption, that what constitutes the 'non-white' population is self-evident and that its interest is equally self-evident, has dominated and continues to dominate discussion about constructing a suitable classification system. In view of this, it is perhaps more appropriate to ascertain what it is about these predetermined populations that distinguishes them in surveys and in analysis which tries to uncover and explain systematic disadvantage. Along these lines it has been forcefully argued that issues of identity and issues of origin should be kept separate: that the Census and other similarly blunt instruments which do not set out to resolve sociological questions of identity are capable of ascertaining the latter, but should not venture into the complex realm of the former.[19] In making such attempts at incorporating aspects of 'identity' they potentially send out problematic messages about identities being mutually exclusive, and also reduce the coherence and therefore analytic potential of the categories.

What is subject to debate is what levels and boundaries of aggregate experience are meaningful and should be employed. The boundaries selected themselves tend to derive from some preconception about what creates different outcomes for different groups of people. Explanation and classification thus feed into each other. To the extent that differences in experience between groups and the overall population and among groups can be distinguished, those classifications can be seen to have a purpose: they invite explanation and amelioration. It is such explanation and suggestions for amelioration that this book offers. That is, the fact that, for example, those who are defined or define themselves as Bangladeshi have an aggregate experience so clearly distinct from the majority justifies classifying Bangladeshis as a group and attempting to look at what factors have a bearing on that experience, whether or not the classification is in reality capturing an ethnic identity strictly defined. It is important to stress that this is not the same as suggesting that the group classification is itself the explanatory factor. Instead, explanation may be sought in a characteristic that is highly associated with such a group. For example, Bangladeshis tend to have larger families than other groups, and larger families are more likely to be in poverty. Hence, an explanation can be developed based on the relation of policy to large families, which indirectly discriminates against Bangladeshis through their family characteristics, rather than one based on their ethnicity *per se*.[20]

'Minority' is used in combination with 'ethnic group' to distinguish those ethnic groups which are small in size relative to the total population and in practice typically distinguishes the 'non-white' groups from the 'white' majority. This book focuses on the experience of those belonging to these groups. It compares their experience with that of the total population. While 'white' is often included in the illustrative tables for completeness, I do not make it the principal point of comparison, since that might imply that the characteristics of the white group constituted the norm to which other groups were being compared. 'Minority', in an additional political sense, refers to the relative powerlessness of those belonging to these groups. In this sense it links into the rationale for this book and the ongoing concern with the disadvantage experienced by particular groups. Those emphasising this usage sometimes prefer to refer to 'minority ethnic groups' (rather than 'ethnic minority groups'). In this book the terms 'ethnic minority group' and 'minority ethnic group' are used interchangeably.

In summary, then, the categories of ethnicity that I work with stand in for a more properly defined 'ethnicity': the categories used can be seen as proxy variables. Chapter 5 says a bit more about who fits into these categories and their histories. A high degree of pragmatism is also necessary, as the categories will themselves vary with the source used. Some surveys combine groups (eg, 'black groups', 'Pakistani and Bangladeshi'); others allow information to be produced at a more disaggregated level. As far as possible, I use the most disaggregated form,[21] with one principal exception. Where black groups are disaggregated, I nevertheless combine the 'black Caribbean' and 'black other' groups as there are good reasons for thinking that these two groups represent to a large extent different generations of a fundamentally comparable minority group population. The younger generation have been shown to be more likely to define themselves as 'black other' or, specifically, as 'black British': a self-definition which is allocated to the 'black other' category. By contrast, the parents of these black British children, particularly if they were themselves born in the Caribbean, are more likely to define themselves as 'black Caribbean'.[22] Where I do this I will refer to the resulting group as 'Caribbean'. 'Black' or 'black groups' will be used to refer to this category when it is further combined with 'black African', though such an aggregation is generally undesirable as it obscures the very different characteristics and trajectories of the Caribbean and African populations. While the black African group is itself clearly a widely various and heterogeneous group, it stands out from the other groups in a number of ways,

which include a very highly educated, but simultaneously very highly disadvantaged profile. A further level of aggregation which is not easily avoid-
ed is the regular incorporation of the Chinese ethnic group into an 'other'
category. As the 'other' group is necessarily a heterogeneous one, representing a variety of experiences, this tends to obscure the characteristics
of the Chinese group, who are notable for their high levels of qualifications
and their relative economic success.

Complete consistency across all the sources employed is, however, virtually impossible to attain. Table 2.1 summarises the different categories used in a range of sources and also distinguishes between those
that are collected and those according to which breakdowns are available
in the published data. Obviously, as well as issues of consistency across
sources and problems of aggregation, there are issues around what is
simply left out in the principal data sources. For example, many studies
have highlighted the peculiarly disadvantaged position of those of Irish origin.[23] However, neither the Census nor the main sources of data on ethnic groups' experience, discussed below, differentiate an Irish ethnic
group. Similarly, many ethnic groups which have distinct profiles and particular concentrations are occluded in much ethnic minority analysis, for
example Turks, Southern Europeans, those from the Middle East, those
from North Africa and those from central and Eastern Europe, in particular Gypsies or Roma. Equally, some of the ethnic group classifications
which are used will contain a number of disparate national or regional
identities, with particular migration histories and/or social, economic and
demographic characteristics. Examples here would be Somali refugees
incorporated into a black African category, Mirpuris, incorporated into a
Pakistani category, or Vietnamese split between a Chinese ethno-nation-
al category and an 'other Asian' residual category. In addition, local studies of particular minority groups, even those which are covered by the
standard classifications, may reveal aspects of their experience which are
either unique to the area considered or which cannot be captured in quantitative sources.[24] This highlights the ongoing need for local data sources,
which can do justice to the subtlety and complexity of ethnic minority con-
figurations and experiences. There is also a need for continuing qualitative
work that both highlights the experience of groups not included in standard classifications and also continues to interrogate the meaning of classifications as people use them or as they are applied to others.

As the main form of immigration in the UK now is from those seeking asylum, a further population about which greater information would be
advantageous is that of refugees, and in particular, asylum seekers who

Table 2.1

Categories used to classify ethnic groups, by source and date

Survey	How collected	Groups classified
Census 1991	Tick box and write in description for 'Other' options.	White, Bangladeshi, Black Caribbean, Black African, Indian, Pakistani, Chinese. Specification of Black-Other and Other resulted in the reallocation of responses to one of the original options or allocation to one of a final three 'other' categories: Black-Other, Other-Asian and Other-Other.
Fourth National Survey of Ethnic Minorities 1993	Options offered in interview on 'family origins' and 'ethnic group'.	*Family origins*: White, Black Caribbean, Indian Caribbean, Indian, Pakistani, Bangladeshi, Chinese, Other, Mixed. *Ethnic group* used the 1991 Census categories. Combined information from these to create White, Caribbean, Indian, African Asian, Pakistani, Bangladeshi and Chinese groups.
Labour Force Survey 1984 and onwards	Options offered in interview with prompts to clarify Black Other and Other, when chosen (1992-2001) or Mixed (2001 onwards).	1981 to 1991 country of origin. From 1992, 1991 Census categories, as above, plus an Other-Mixed group; but aggregated in most tables to White, Black groups, Indian, Pakistani and Bangladeshi, and Other. From 2001 categories as for 2001 Census.
Family Resources Survey 1994/95 onwards	Options offered in interview.	1991 Census categories but aggregated to White, Black groups (or sometimes Black Caribbean and Black non-Caribbean), Pakistani and Bangladeshi, Indian, and Other in published material.
2001 Census (and now official Office for National Statistics categories)	Tick box with write in description for 'Other' options	White (British, Other White), Mixed (White and Black Caribbean; White and Black African; White and Asian; Other Mixed), Asian or Asian British (Indian; Pakistani; Bangladeshi; Other Asian), Black or Black British (Caribbean; African; Other Black), Chinese, and Other.

have not yet achieved a formal status. This is of especial concern given the Home Office's attempts to discourage those it perceives to be 'economic migrants' by systematically limiting the resources available to asylum seekers, an issue discussed further in Chapter 6.

A final issue relating to the provision of information about ethnic minority groups' experience is the demographic unit from which ethnicity is derived. The most relevant facts relating to ethnic minority poverty are those which can tell us about the number of individuals in each minority group. Sometimes, however, information will be provided about households headed by a member of a particular group or about those individuals living in a household headed by a member of a particular group – whose ethnicity all individuals may not share. In addition, the *Family Resources Survey* provides information not just about 'households' but also about 'benefit units' (the immediate family of an individual, her/his partner, if any, and dependent children, if any). Again, information provided according to the ethnicity of the benefit unit 'head' may disguise the multiple ethnicities that may make up the unit. On the other hand, the fact of the ethnicity of the head of household or benefit unit may be the critical issue in determining the welfare of the rest of the family, regardless of variations in the ethnicity of the other family members.[25]

Poverty measurement

The meaning and definition of poverty is a long debated and highly contested question.[26] Here, I outline some of the measures that have been employed to assess its extent. First, however, it is worth considering briefly what it is that such measures are trying to capture. Townsend famously and influentially described poverty in the following way:

> 'Poverty can be defined objectively and applied consistently only in terms of the concept of relative deprivation... The term is understood objectively rather than subjectively. Individuals, families and groups in the population can be said to be in poverty when they lack the resources to obtain the types of diet, participate in the activities and have the living conditions and amenities which are customary, or are at least widely encouraged or approved, in the societies to which they belong. Their resources are so seriously below those commanded by the average individual or family that they are, in effect, excluded from ordinary living patterns, customs and activities.'[27]

Despite criticisms of Townsend's method of ascertaining the existence of such poverty, including his notion of 'average' individual lives and what is meant by 'ordinary living patterns',[28] his approach was important in relating poverty to particular experiences and lacks: not having a winter coat, not being able to have children's friends round. It also stressed the effects of poverty on social relations and citizenship, and that poverty was related to social norms. That is, deprivation is relational and may vary with varying expectations and social norms. These points are all relevant to the discussion of poverty measures that follows. First, it is important not to lose sight of what poverty means, both at a material and social level. Poverty means not being able to keep warm in winter, but it also impacts on many other aspects of life. It has implications for health, for residence, for education, for the ability to make and sustain relationships, for community participation. Second, poverty is necessarily relative – relative to prevailing norms and living standards, though how we judge which norms are important and which living standards form the basis for comparison is a problematic question. Third, poverty constitutes a form of exclusion from the exercise of citizenship, for participating in society in the ways that we might expect or that might be expected of us.

There follows a discussion of the principal poverty measures that are or have been used and their strengths and weaknesses. These measures are considered in relation to minority groups' experiences of poverty in Chapter 3.

Households Below Average Income

One of the most straightforward and therefore widely used measures of poverty is to set a poverty line or income threshold in relation to the middle of the income distribution and to count the number or percentage of persons (or households) with incomes below that line. Thus, thresholds of 50 per cent of average (mean) income or 60 per cent of median (the mid-point) income are regularly employed, with all those below such points being counted as poor.[29] This is the approach employed in the Department for Work and Pensions' *Households Below Average Income (HBAI)* annual series. In the Government's *Opportunity for All* targets, a range of fractions of mean and median are cited, though the preference is to employ 60 per cent of the median.[30] In practice, 60 per cent of the median and 50 per cent of the mean represent very similar values and thus can be seen as an almost interchangeable measure.[31] The advantages of such a line are that it is easy to calculate when the overall income distribution is known and that comparison over time of the number of people falling below the line is simple. Criticisms stem from the fact that the real income level that constitutes average income varies over time and thus the measure is informative about inequality rather than poverty *per se*. One way round this is to adopt a fixed fraction of income for a given year and then to examine who falls below this line in real income terms in subsequent years. This approach is also adopted in the *HBAI* series and in the *Opportunity for All* indicators. This provides a stationary measure of poverty, though it is still not immune to the criticism that it is an arbitrary one. On the other hand, there are those who would argue that inequalities and the growth in the number of those removed from the average standard of living or the distance by which they are divorced from such average standards questions any expectation that they can participate meaningfully in society, and that, therefore, inequality measures form appropriate poverty indicators. In practice, the ease of reproduction and comprehension of measuring poverty based on fixed fraction of average income, alongside the fact that it enables comparison, makes it the preferred measure for much applied poverty research as well as the basis of political statements and the formulation of policy.[32]

Descriptions of the income distribution in *HBAI* allocate households to certain parts of the distribution both on the basis of their incomes before housing costs (BHC) and after housing costs (AHC). This is on account of the fact that housing costs are a committed expenditure. Those who have high housing costs will look better off than their actual disposable income allows in the BHC figures and those who have low housing costs will look worse off than available income suggests. Thus income after housing costs may be seen as a better measure. On the other hand, if low housing costs reflect poor quality of accommodation, itself associated with low income, then measures after housing costs might imply a higher income for some households than their actual quality of life suggests, and thus income before housing costs might be seen as more relevant.[33] In the tables in Chapter 3 derived from *HBAI*, the figures quoted are after housing costs only.[34]

All incomes for households or families in the *HBAI* are equivalised; that is, they are adjusted to take account of household size and composition. Thus, a family of four living off a given income will be deemed to have a lower *equivalent* income than a single person on the same actual income since, in the former case, the resources will have to meet the needs of four people rather than one. *HBAI* adjusts actual incomes to allow for the demands made upon those incomes and thus cites 'equivalent' incomes. It makes the adjustments using a scale, the McClement's scale, which takes account of both the number of persons and also the lower costs of children at younger ages. It treats a couple as the reference point, thus the equivalent income of a couple will be the same as their real income. There are two versions of the McClement's scale: one adjusts incomes before housing costs and the other provides adjustments which apply to incomes after housing costs. Discussions of income in other publications will also be referring, as a matter of course, to equivalent incomes. Many use the McClement's scale for adjusting incomes; others will use alternative ways of adjusting incomes, sometimes on the grounds that the McClement's scale weights the costs of children rather low.

Budget standards

A different approach to measuring poverty is to calculate what people need to survive by using a 'budget standards' approach. Here, a 'basket of goods' that represents the minimum to avoid poverty, including housing, heating and transport costs and so on for different types of household is costed and the poverty line is then set at this level of 'subsistence'. People or households are then deemed to be poor if their income falls below this line, rendering them unable to fund such a 'basket'. Though this approach often matches to people's intuitive sense of how to estimate poverty, it is a costly and lengthy process to produce the measure, a measure which becomes out of date as lifestyles (and costs) change and therefore both what are perceived as necessities and their value alters. Such budget standards estimates were more common in the early days of poverty research.[35] Recent work on these lines has been carried out by Jonathan Bradshaw and colleagues, by Sue Middleton and others and by Hermione Parker and others.[36] Such work can provide a valuable point of comparison for benefit levels, and for illuminating the costs of low-income living, but is not easy to apply in other situations and is not amenable to looking at change over time. Such work tries to estimate the income that any family would need in order to provide for necessities, though acknowledging that families would not, in reality, spend their money in exactly the way that the budget calculates. While such an acknowledgement leads to a consideration of those who would still therefore be lacking necessities through 'misapplication' of their income, it also allows for the possibility of

different choices in spending. Those above the income threshold would
be regarded as being able to make culturally diverse spending decisions
and yet still remain out of poverty, while those below the income threshold would be in poverty regardless of spending patterns. Thus these
budget standards do not, of themselves, presuppose or exclude a consideration of the income and poverty of groups who may buy different
sorts of food or clothing.

Deprivation of necessities

A further way to measure poverty is to take deprivation as the core element, rather than attempting to gauge an income level. Peter Townsend
conceived of poverty as the inability to participate in normal life due to
being deprived of a number of socially endorsed 'necessities', which
could be both commodities (a warm winter coat) or activities (the ability to
entertain or celebrate birthdays or to have children's friends round).[37]

Poverty as the absence of popularly endorsed 'necessities' was a
measure that was pursued by Mack and Lansley's *Breadline Britain* investigations.[38] These claimed to operate a consensual approach, though crit-
ics highlighted the arbitrary nature of deciding what number of missing
essentials constituted poverty and also what proportion of the population
had to endorse an essential for it to be 'consensually' regarded as such.
A necessity that has been endorsed by more than 50 per cent of the population may have been rejected by 45 per cent. And, like the budget standards approach, there is also the issue that 'necessities' change with
time. Deprivation has also been employed as a poverty measure in a number of other studies, based on information from existing surveys.[39] Here
the items are not socially determined, but are selected by the investigators
from those available within the original survey design. In these studies, it
is the absence of specific 'goods' which primarily determines the absence
or presence of poverty as deprivation. But in such studies, as in Mack and
Lansley's work or more recently that of Gordon and others, the existence
of deprivation (rather than unusual lifestyle choices) is confirmed by cross-
checking it with income data.[40] The primacy of income in determining
poverty, therefore, tends to be confirmed.

Investigations of deprivation using a consensual measure have not
been able to provide breakdowns by ethnic group of those deprived of
two or more necessities. Had it been possible to do so, it would perhaps
have raised further questions about the extent to which the approach was

appropriate to an understanding of deprivation among different minority ethnic groups. This is not to assume that minority groups have totally distinct lifestyles. Such an argument could lead to suggestions of different poverty thresholds for different groups, which, while an interesting issue to explore in another context, would negate the minority group/population comparisons, which are the subject of this book. The purpose here is to explore the extent to which poverty, as a condition that separates those experiencing it from the quality of life of the population as a whole, is suffered more by some groups than by others. Thus, population levels of, and expectations of, standards of living are highly relevant. Nevertheless, the acknowledgement of different groups implies that there are differences between them. Some part of this may be cultural differences, and different choices and expectations; some part of this may be in terms of systematic differences in experience of life. And in fact, the two cannot be separated since, just as cultural factors will affect outcomes across a whole range of living experiences, including probabilities of poverty, experience will also shape aspirations, expectations and apparently cultural patterns of living, an issue explored further in Chapter 4. The reason the consensual measure is problematic is, therefore, that each necessity requires endorsement from 50 per cent or more of the population. Items could be endorsed by quite specific groups of the population, and could be rejected as necessities by nearly half the population.[41] This raises questions about the extent to which they may be relevant to all people. Equally, aspects of life that are of significant importance to substantial numbers of the population may be excluded from consideration as necessities by such a measure. The attempt to understand deprivation and what it means in people's lives is an extremely important one. There would, however, seem to be problems in conflating the experience or consequences of poverty with its definition, and these problems are intensified when we try to uncover the particularity of ethnic group poverty.

In the particular field of minority group poverty, income-based measures have, I would argue, a transparency that makes them more appropriate than deprivation measures. There is already a danger that 'cultural' arguments are used to explain differences in outcomes for minority ethnic groups at the expense of structural ones.[42] At the same time, a 'consensual' approach to measurement may ill fit the specific context of particular minority groups' experience. Hence, measures of poverty based on 'expert' or majority views on 'normal' standards of living hold within them the potential *either* to explain away *or* to misrepresent minority groups' poverty. An income definition in its simplicity does not take into account what people do with their money (either by choice or constraint), nor does it make room for judging the poverty of different groups differently. While it is, therefore, not sensitive to possible cultural factors in the experience of poverty, including extra costs associated with, say, religious practices, it avoids the indiscriminate ascription of particular behaviours to particular groups. Rather, an income-based measure of poverty fits with the rationale of this book, in that it is the observed differences in experience and outcome between groups that enable us to consider what the role of ethnicity is in the process.

Social exclusion

The measurement of poverty as deprivation and as inequality has also become linked in recent years to ideas of social exclusion and the importance of social exclusion rather than of income *per se* to life choices and chances. Many of the attempts at defining or summarising what social exclusion means draw on ideas of deprivation and non-participation, or, conversely, define inclusion in relation to participation. Thus we find that social exclusion is described in the following way in *Opportunity for All*:

> 'Social exclusion and poverty are terms that are often used interchangeably. However, there are some further dimensions to the concept of social exclusion. The Prime Minister described social exclusion as
>
> 'A short-hand label for what can happen when individuals or areas suffer from a combination of linked problems such as unemployment, poor skills, low incomes, poor housing, high crime environments, bad health and family breakdown.'
>
> As this suggests, social exclusion occurs where different factors combine to trap individuals and areas in a spiral of disadvantage. Confronting these combinations of negative factors requires an integrated and radical policy response.'[43]

Conversely the image of a society free from the shadow of social exclusion is expressed in reverse terms:

> 'We are committed to tackling poverty, promoting social inclusion and increasing opportunity for all. We are determined to create a United

Kingdom where everyone has opportunities to work, to learn, to make a contribution and to achieve their full potential. We are aiming for a society where everyone is able to enjoy the benefits of economic prosperity and to participate in community life. Our goal is for a fairer society; one where no child lives in poverty.'[44]

Thus, while the idea of social exclusion goes beyond an income-based understanding of poverty, it is closely allied to received wisdom on the *consequences* of poverty, in particular long-term consequences over one or more generations.[45] It has also been argued elsewhere that income inequality itself acts to exclude people socially and that exclusion can be understood in relation to standard measures of income poverty and income inequality:

> 'The familiar form of social exclusion affects those who are unable to partic-
> ipate in the institutions patronised by the majority. There is also, however,
> exclusion of the majority by a minority who are in a position to opt out of the
> mainstream institutions: the epitome of this is the 'gated community' .... [F]or
> a society such as that of Britain, it seems plausible that to avoid the social
> exclusion of a minority it is necessary for nobody to have less than half tho
> median income, and that to avoid the social exclusion of the majority it is
> necessary for only a few to have more than three times the median
> income.'[46]

The idea of social exclusion draws on previous concepts such as the under-class and cycles of disadvantage and 'inner city' deprivation, which them-selves have tended to have an association with minority ethnicity and the entrenched disadvantage of certain minority ethnic groups.[47] Thus, when attempting to chart ethnic minority poverty and its causes and conse-quences, as this book does, ideas associated with social exclusion will tend to recur, but can also serve to confuse the issues under consideration.

Means-tested benefits

Finally, an indication of poverty levels can be found through counts of recipients of means-tested benefits. Means-tested benefits are now no longer commonly used as a *measure* of poverty, but the number and con-centration of recipients continue to be used as indicators of poverty. Benefit receipt or the value of benefit levels, nevertheless, have a history of use as a poverty measure and continue to provide evidence of the extent of income poverty and who is income poor. Townsend used 140 per cent of supplementary benefit as one of his poverty lines in *Poverty in the United Kingdom*, on the basis, he argued, that this took into account not only the basic value of supplementary benefit but also the discretionary payments that were regularly paid in addition.[48] The Government's *Low Income Families* series (which came to an end in 1985) adopted this threshold of 140 per cent of basic supplementary benefit for its analysis of those living on a low income. Receipt of income support, which replaced supplementary benefit in 1988 and which no longer retained the discretionary elements, has also on occasions been used as a measure of poverty. This use has been criticised on the grounds that an increase in generosity of the benefit will result in an apparent increase in poverty. However, such an argument about more generous benefits reveals an assumption that comparison over time is the essential criterion for poverty measurement and is more important than refining the concept of what basic needs actually are and how much they cost to meet. As long as income support levels do not exceed what is deemed to be an appropriate poverty level – and budget standards work has tended to demonstrate that this is far from the case[49] – then it is not inappropriate to regard it as one, typically low, threshold and to analyse the composition of the claimant population accordingly.

Table 2.2

Income support rates 1999/00 and 2000/01 and HBAI 60 per cent of median values, 1999/00 and 2000/01

	Income support 1999/00 £	HBAI 60% of median threshold 1999/00 £	Income support as % of HBAI low income threshold	Income support 2000/01 £	HBAI 60% of median threshold 2000/01 £	Income support as % of HBAI low income threshold
Single people						
Aged 18-24 (or lone parents aged under 18)	40.70	80.85	50%	41.35	84.15	49%
Aged over 25 (or lone parents aged over 18)	51.40	80.85	64%	52.20	84.15	62%

Couples						
Aged 18 or over	80.65	147.00	55%	81.95	153.00	54%
Children						
Under 11	20.20	10.29 to 33.81	196%– 60%	30.95	10.71 to 35.19	289%– 88%
11-15	25.90	38.22 to 41.16	68%– 63%	30.95	39.78 to 42.84	78%– 72%
16-18	30.95	55.86	55%	31.75	58.14	55%
Family premium	13.90	–	–	14.25	–	–
Sample families						
Couple with child aged 4	114.75	173.46	66%	127.15	180.54	70%
Couple with children aged 4 and 14	140.65	214.16	66%	158.10	223.38	71%
Couple with children aged 4, 10 and 14	160.85	248.43	65%	189.05	258.57	73%
Lone parent with child aged 4	85.50	107.31	80%	97.4	111.69	87%
Lone parent with children aged 4 and 14	111.40	148.47	75%	128.35	154.53	83%

Source: Department for Work and Pensions, *A Guide to Benefits*, 1999 and 2000 and author's analysis from Department for Work and Pensions, *Households Below Average Income 1999/00*, and *Households Below Average Income 2000/01*. The 60 per cent of median values have been calculated using the McClement's After Housing Costs Equivalence Scale, and including self-employment incomes.

Table 2.2.gives a condensed version of the values of income support rates for the years 1999/00 and 2000/01, the years corresponding to much of the data cited in this book. It also compares the values with 60 per cent of median income thresholds for the same years to ascertain the extent to which income support levels fall below this standard low-income measure. And it compares the totals for a selection of family compositions – since the direct comparison does not take account of the income support family premium where children are present. The comparisons are made using the median *after* housing costs, since those on income support typically have their housing costs funded through housing and council tax benefits.

As Table 2.2 illustrates, income support levels remain well below the

Government's preferred low-income threshold of 60 per cent of the median. As the values for sample families show, the family premium and the increases in allowances for younger children mean that family incomes have more nearly approached the *HBAI* threshold. Nevertheless, they still remain at only around 70 to 80 per cent of the low income cut-off. The higher proportions of the 60 per cent of median received by lone parents reveals the low weight accorded to the partner in a couple in income support rates.

The increasing availability of income support claimant counts at small levels of aggregation means that benefit data can be particularly suitable for assessing geographical concentrations of poverty, which survey data cannot do to the same extent. For example, income support or income-based jobseeker's allowance receipt has been used as one component of the 2000 Indices of Deprivation.[50] On the other hand, ethnic group information is not currently collected for claimants of nationally administered benefits.[51] It cannot, therefore, give us measures for ethnic minority poverty. However, the locally administered means-tested benefits, housing benefit and council tax benefit, do, on occasion, contain ethnic group information, and therefore in such cases breakdowns at local authority level do become possible for these benefits. Such information can be highly informative about patterns of poverty, particularly where the local authority is sufficiently large and has a large minority group population, as recent work on Birmingham has shown.[52]

A final criticism levelled at benefit receipt as a measure of poverty is that it misses those who are eligible for but not receiving the benefit, and who are thus subsisting at a level below benefit rates but are not recognised as such.[53] The issue of non-take-up of benefit remains a problem for benefit-based poverty measurement. However, it would appear to be a diminishing one as take-up rates improve, though the robustness of take-up estimates themselves are currently being externally assessed and recalculated, and the introduction of new benefits typically brings with it problems of take-up. Nevertheless, there is room for further work investigating whether ethnicity is a factor in under-claiming, an issue to which we will return in Chapter 6.

Child poverty

While this is not a book specifically about child poverty, it highlights issues of child poverty at a number of points in the discussion, including the descriptive account of minority ethnic groups' poverty that makes up Chapter 3. There are a number of reasons for this. First is the widely endorsed acknowledgement that child poverty is an issue of crucial importance. Tony Blair's pledge to end child poverty within a generation is both widely cited and is only regarded as contentious in the length of the projected time scale.[54] Second is the fact that, while child poverty rates are high compared to overall poverty rates, the extent of child poverty among minority ethnic groups, particularly among black Africans, Pakistanis and Bangladeshis is of shocking proportions. Third is the fact that it is children who contain the futures of the minority ethnic groups. To the extent that these children are growing up in poverty the prospects for the groups are a cause for concern, independent of obstacles that they may face later on in life.

Government endorsed measures of poverty

The Labour administration which came to power in 1997 reversed the denial of poverty that had typified the preceding Conservative governments. Instead, in its *Opportunity for All* documents it acknowledged problems of poverty and social exclusion and set targets for improvement.[55] In order to measure progress towards the targets, it identified indicators. Therefore, while there is not an official measure of poverty in Britain in the sense that, for example, the US has an official poverty line, there is an acceptance of certain measures for providing indications of diminution or increase of low income among the adult and child populations. For the target of improving family incomes it uses low-income indicators of the:

- proportions of children, of working-age adults and of pensioners below various fractions of both mean and median contemporary income;
- proportions of children, of working-age adults and of pensioners below various fractions of both mean and median income held constant in real terms at 1996/97 levels; *and*

- proportions of children, of working-age adults and of pensioners below 60 or 70 per cent of median income for any three out of four years.

For working-age adults it also has an indicator of the numbers living in families supported by income support or income-based jobseeker's allowance for two or more years. There are a number of targets specifi-cally for communities and for narrowing the gap between the most deprived areas and the rest of the country using measures of employ-ment, housing conditions, burglary and life expectancy. Overall, the pre-ferred low-income indicator of those offered is that of those below 60 per cent of the median. *Opportunity for All* has no specific income targets for members of minority ethnic groups, although it does have a target for increasing the rates of employment among those of working-age from minority groups. Here, though, the indicators aggregate all minority groups and thus fail to distinguish the differences in rates by group – and by gender within groups – or whether progress is being made by all groups equally.

In 2002, there was a government consultation on child poverty that proposed four options for measuring child poverty measurement. The options were:

- multi-dimensional headline indicators, drawn from the *Opportunity for All* indicators;
- a child poverty index combining the headline indicators to produce a single figure;
- a headline measure of consistent poverty, combining relative low income and material deprivation;
- a core set of indicators of low income and consistent poverty.[56]

There is, therefore, clearly a continuing recognition both that the *HBAI* low-income measures do not measure the complex reality of poverty – 'that poverty is about far more than income'[57] – and that child poverty measurement may require a particular approach. It also stresses the impact of growing up in a deprived area on children's outcomes.[58] There is, however, no reference to children from minority ethnic group families or whether any of these measures may be more or less appropriate to such children.

Social class

A crucial contribution to understanding the differences in experience and outcome *between* minority ethnic groups has been the exploration of the contribution of social class and social class background. While both the meaning accorded to social class and the means by which it is measured vary throughout the literature and have been a source of extensive long-standing debate,[59] it provides a valuable tool for understanding the minority ethnic group experience and some of its determinants. In this book social class is used to convey an understanding of occupational position, which often goes hand in hand with the possession of social or human capital, that is the knowledge, contacts and information that makes certain, more prestigious occupations more accessible and occupational success more likely.

Classes have regularly been measured according to a five class occupational scheme, known as the registrar general's classification. This is still most commonly used for analysis of occupations or for relating social class to outcomes such as health outcomes. It has, however, recently been revised following the development of a new classification system called the National Statistics Socio-economic Classification (or NS-SEC), based on occupation and employment contract that is more pertinent to today's occupations and which enables a class classification to be allocated to the non-employed.[60] This revised classification will replace the former class schema in official sources. Another commonly used measure is Goldthorpe's class schema, which was influential in the construction of the new NS-SEC.[61] All these classifications are susceptible to a crude regrouping which distinguishes working class, intermediate class and middle class backgrounds. While social class is regularly associated with income it is distinct from measures of income or poverty and is more concerned with the *potentiality* offered by the class background and the sorts of characteristics that can be anticipated to go with it than with income *per se*. On the one hand, therefore, it can indicate situations in which ethnic minority outcomes can be explained more in terms of their class rather than ethnicity. On the other hand, comparing the experience of ethnic groups within classes can more potently reveal some of the obstacles they face and the operation of discrimination within institutions, insofar as earnings differentials are greater for some groups at higher occupational levels.

An understanding of class in relation to possession of human capital rather than in terms of current position can also give some insights into why, for example, the children of East African Asian forced migrants achieve well relative to their parents, as they tend to reflect their parents' implicit, rather than achieved, occupational class. On the other hand, as this example also shows, occupational class measurements may fail to capture the educational and aspirational background which may influence achievement in the children's generation even where the parents' generation has, through discrimination or the negative impacts of migration failed to achieve their true class position. Social class, therefore, has an important role to play in understanding ethnic minority groups' outcomes. But its use also has to be treated with caution where the measures of class may not be accurately capturing the background factors for which they are intended.

Sources

The principal quantitative sources that help to inform us about the patterns of ethnic minority poverty in Britain and its possible causes are outlined below. This is not to downplay the role of more qualitative sources of information. Such sources have drawn attention to many pertinent issues and continue to provide both a more detailed and sensitive understanding of the experience of ethnic minorities in poverty and also to bring new issues to the fore. The relevant literature is drawn upon throughout this book. Here, rather, the purpose is to highlight data sources from which we can obtain a generalised overview of the situations of members of minority ethnic groups – and which are used in this book to provide such an overview – at the same time as indicating some of their limitations.

The *Family Resources Survey* is run by the Department for Work and Pensions (DWP) in order to 'support the monitoring of the social security programme; support the costing and modelling of changes to national insurance contributions and social security benefits; and provide better information for the forecasting of benefit expenditure'.[62] It is an annual survey that has run since 1993/94, and that uses multi-stage stratified random sampling to achieve a representative sample of around 25,000 households from Great Britain each year. It collects information on family structure and ethnic group, tenure and housing costs, consumer durables, occupation and employment, wages and self-employed earnings, pensions and benefits, and other sources of income. Until 1994 the government had no national information on low-income distributions by ethnic group. The substitution of the *Family Resources Survey* for the smaller *Family Expenditure Survey*, which did not collect ethnic group information for the production of *HBAI* series, meant that such information became available. The most recent published tables from the *Family Resources Survey* and from *HBAI* are drawn upon in this book to provide contextual and validating information for the analysis, and some secondary sources that draw on various years of the survey are also used.

The *Fourth National Survey of Ethnic Minorities* 1993/94 is the fourth in a series of decennial surveys that have investigated Britain's minority populations since the 1960s. It aims to provide a representative picture of the lives and experiences of people from specific minority ethnic groups in Britain. The survey covered England and Wales, and used multi-stage stratified sampling techniques to identify and interview 5,196 adults (living in around 3,500 households) from Caribbean, Indian, Pakistani, Bangladeshi or Chinese family origins. From the South Asian groups it derived a sixth East African Asian group (identified through their place of birth or former residence). It used a comparison sample of 2,867 white respondents to compare with the responses of the main sample. It collected information on a range of subjects including health, education and attitudes. For the purposes of this book the information that is of most relevance is that on economic status and income (including sources of income) combined with the information on the family characteristics of the respondents. The findings of the survey, as published in 1997, are drawn upon for these topics and for information on minority ethnic groups' education and employment status.[63] Given the way the minority ethnic groups were classified the survey cannot be *directly* compared with the other sources used, but nevertheless, despite its age, it continues to provide invaluable contextual information.

The *Labour Force Survey* is a government survey of around 60,000 households, carried out on a quarterly basis. Results are typically aggregated across four quarters to give annual estimates. Households are re-contacted for five consecutive quarters before they are replaced by a new sample. The survey covers economic activity, occupation, hours, pay, job search and so on, as well as a number of 'background' questions including ethnic group. The ethnic group questions were based on the 1991 Census categories from 1992 but have recently changed to the 2001 Census categories (see Table 2.1).

The *1991 Census* is now over a decade old, but the information from the 2001 Census is not yet available, and the 1991 Census was the first in which an ethnic group question was asked. It thus provided an unprecedented source of information on the exact size, demography, geographical distribution, tenure, family forms and employment of Britain's minority ethnic group populations. For some types of information it still constitutes the best and most detailed source, particularly where information about smaller minority groups or sub-national areas is sought. It contained no income information, but is highly relevant when attempting to explore possible *causes* of minority group poverty such as occupation or family size. It also forms the basis of more recent population estimates, though the most recent population estimates are based on the new (2001) ethnic group classification rather than the 1991 one.

The *Youth Cohort Survey* provides information annually on qualifications and post-compulsory education status of 16–18-year-olds. It collects information on social class, gender and ethnic group and provides a useful source to compare the outcomes across cohorts of school leavers. Unfortunately, however, there are insufficient numbers of respondents from black groups to enable reliable estimates of their outcomes and educational achievements. This limits its utility in making comparisons between ethnic groups. It nevertheless provides a helpful cross-section of outcomes for the age groups, how they differ from parents' social class and a number of other factors.

Country and regional coverage

Ethnic minority groups are not evenly distributed across Britain. They all show a numerical preponderance in England, and within England display different patterns of regional concentration and dispersion. Area is therefore a pertinent issue in this book. The sources used relate to different geographical areas and are available at different levels of regional or sub-regional breakdown. For example, the *Fourth National Survey of Ethnic Minorities* covered only England and Wales, given the small numbers of minority ethnic group members living in Scotland. Unlike the *Family Expenditure Survey*, which covers the UK, the *Family Resources Survey*, and therefore *HBAI*, covers Great Britain (though excluding the Scottish Highlands and Islands), as does the *Labour Force Survey*. The Census covers Great Britain. In the tables in this book, if the area referred to differs from these total areas covered by the surveys the area referred to is indicated in the title. Population figures are estimated both for Great Britain and for England and Wales, and the geographical area referred to is indicated. The *Family Resources Survey* and *Labour Force Survey* enable regional and sometimes sub-regional breakdowns, while the Census enables residential patterns and concentrations to be investigated to the level of enumeration districts. Any regional breakdowns are noted in the tables.

Timeliness and period

For poverty rates and counts I have used the most recent data available at the time of writing. For *HBAI* and the *Family Resources Survey* this meant using the results of the 2000/01 survey. However, where I have conducted my own breakdowns from *HBAI*, the most recent data released at the time of analysis were from the 1999/00 survey. Population estimates are those for 2001. 2001 Census results on ethnic group populations only begin to be released after this volume goes to press. For all sources, I attempt to find those which give the most up-to-date account, though insights from research dating back ten or more years may well still be pertinent, and may not have been superseded by more recent research. At all times, I have tried to be clear about the period covered by research cited, and the extent to which it can still be deemed to be relevant today.

Notes

1   For a brief account of the heterogeneity of Britain's past, see B Parekh, *The Future of Multi-Ethnic Britain* (The Parekh Report), Profile Books, 2000, pp14-27

2   For a summary of responses to the post-war migration, see J Solomos, *Race and Racism in Contemporary Britain*, Macmillan, 1989

3   *Opportunity for All: tackling poverty and social exclusion*, Cm4445, The Stationary Office, 1999; Social Exclusion Unit, *What is Social Exclusion?*, 2000, available at http://www.cabinet-office.gov.uk/seu/index/

4   T Modood, *It's Not Easy Being British: colour, culture and citizenship*, Trentham Books, 1992; T Modood 'Employment' in T Modood, R Berthoud *et al*, *Ethnic Minorities in Britain: diversity and disadvantage*, Policy Studies Institute, 1997, pp130-134. See also the discussion in B Parekh, *The Future of Multi-Ethnic Britain* (The Parekh Report), Profile Books, 2000, pp61-62

5   For fuller discussions of race and racism than this section allows, see M Banton,

Racial Theories, Cambridge University Press, 1998; P Gilroy, *There ain't no Black in the Union Jack: the cultural politics of race and nation*, Hutchinson, 1987; P Gilroy, *Between Camps: nations, cultures and the allure of race*, Penguin, 2000; D Mason, *Race and Ethnicity in Modern Britain*, Oxford University Press, 1995; J Solomos, *Race and Racism in Contemporary Britain*, Macmillan, 1989; P Ratcliffe, *'Race', Ethnicity and Nation*, UCL Press, 1994; P Ratcliffe, *The Politics of Social Science Research: 'race', ethnicity and social change*, Palgrave, 2001

6   For a discussion of this issue, see D Rose, 'The Continuing Significance of Race? Teaching ethnic and racial studies in sociology' in M Bulmer and J Solmos (eds), *Ethnic and Racial Studies Today*, Routledge, 1999

7   B Parekh, *The Future of Multi-Ethnic Britain* (The Parekh Report), Profile Books, 2000, p57

8   Though see S Virdee, *Racial Violence and Harassment*, Policy Studies Institute, 1995

9   Commission for Racial Equality, *The Race Relations Act 1976*, 1999, at http://www.cre.gov.uk/law/rra76.html (accessed 21 November 2000)

10 W Macpherson, *The Stephen Lawrence Inquiry: report of an inquiry by Sir William Macpherson of Cluny*, The Stationery Office, 1999

11 D Coleman and J Salt, 'The Ethnic Group Question in the 1991 Census of Population: a new landmark in British social statistics' in *Ethnicity in the 1991 Census: Volume one: demographic characteristics of the ethnic minority populations*, OPCS, 1996, p12

12 R Skellington, *'Race' in Britain Today*, Sage, 1996, pp24-25

13 For a stringent criticism of the 1991 ethnic group question, see R Ballard 'The Construction of a Conceptual Vision: 'ethnic groups' and the 1991 UK Census' in *Ethnic and Racial Studies* 20, 1991, pp182-194; further discussion can be found in P Ratcliffe, 'Social Geography and Ethnicity: a theoretical, conceptual and substantive overview' in *Ethnicity in the 1991 Census: Volume Three: social geography and ethnicity in Britain: geographical spread, spatial concentration and internal migration*, HMSO, 1996; and a rationalisation of the question can be found in M Bulmer, 'The Ethnic Group Question in the 1991 Census of Population' in D Coleman and J Salt (eds) *Ethnicity in the 1991 Census: Volume One: demographic characteristics of the ethnic minority populations*, HMSO, 1996

14 See for example, G Craig, 'Race and New Labour' in G Fimister (ed), *An End in Sight? Tackling child poverty in the UK*, CPAG, 2001, p92; see also National Statistics' discussion and justification of the new classification, 'The Classification of Ethnic Groups' at http://www.statistics.gov.uk/themes/compendia_reference/articles/ns_ethnic_classification.asp

15 See P Ratcliffe, 'Social Geography and Ethnicity: a theoretical, conceptual and substantive overview' in *Ethnicity in the 1991 Census: Volume three: social geography and ethnicity in Britain: geographical spread, spatial concentration and internal migration*, ONS, 1996, p5

16 See note 7

17 See note 4

18 M Weber, *Economy and Society*, edited by G Roth and C Wittach, University of California Press, 1978, p389; R A Schermerhorn, *Comparative Ethnic Relations: a framework for theory and research*, University of Chicago Press, 1978, p12

19 R Berthoud, 'Defining Ethnic Groups: origin or identity?' *Patterns of Prejudice*, 32, 1998

20 J Nazroo in *The Health of Britain's Ethnic Minorities: findings from a national survey*, Policy Studies Institute, 1997 has pointed out the fallacy of attempting to explain ethnic health differentials through cultural factors crudely identified with the ethnic group.

21 Including, where necessary, reanalysis of *Households Below Average Income* data.

22 D Owen, 'Black Other: the melting pot' in C Peach (ed), *Ethnicity in the 1991 Census: Volume two: the ethnic minority populations of Great Britain*, HMSO, 1996; T Warnes, 'The Age Structure and Ageing of the Ethnic Groups' in D Coleman and J Salt (eds), *Ethnicity in the 1991 Census: Volume one: demographic characteristics of the ethnic minority populations*, HMSO, 1996; T Modood, R Berthoud *et al*, *Ethnic Minorities in Britain: diversity and disadvantage*, Policy Studies Institute, 1997; R Berthoud, *The Incomes of Ethnic Minorities*, ISER, University of Essex, 1998

23 See for example, the summary in Birmingham City Council, *The Irish in Birmingham: a community profile*, 1996

24 See for example, A Dale, E Fieldhouse, N Shaheen and V Kalra, 'The Labour Market Prospects for Pakistani and Bangladeshi Women', *Work, Employment and Society* 16.1, 2002; E McFarland, M Dalton and D Walsh, 'Ethnic Minority Needs and Service Delivery: the barriers to access in a Glasgow inner-city area', *New Community* 15, 1989; P Ratcliffe, *'Race' and Housing in Bradford: addressing the needs of South Asian, African and Caribbean communities*, Bradford Housing Forum, 1996; A Brah and S Shaw, *Working Choices: South Asian young Muslim women and the labour market*, Department of Employment Research Paper 61, 1992; F Edholm, H Roberts and J Sayer, *Vietnamese Refugees in Britain*, Commission for Racial Equality, 1983

25 In the text, for reasons of simplicity I refer to what are technically 'benefit units' as families. I note in relation to any tables based on such 'families' that this use implies the restricted family of the 'benefit unit'.

26 For overviews of the issues, see P Alcock, *Understanding Poverty*, Macmillan, 1993; J Bradshaw and R Sainsbury (eds), *Researching Poverty*, Ashgate, 2000; J Bradshaw, 'The Nature of Poverty' in J Ditch (ed), *Introduction to Social Security: policies, benefits and poverty*, Routledge, 1999; and Chapter 1 in M Howard, A Garnham, G Fimister and J Veit-Wilson, *Poverty: the facts*, CPAG, 2001

27 P Townsend, *Poverty in the United Kingdom: a survey of household resources and standards of living*, Penguin, 1979, p31

28 For example, D Piachaud, 'Peter Townsend and the Holy Grail', *New Society* 57, pp419-421

29 For example, these two measures are used in tandem in M Howard, A Garnham, G Fimister and J Veit-Wilson, *Poverty: the facts*, CPAG, 2001

30 Department for Work and Pensions, *Opportunity for All – Making Progress*, Cm 5260, September 2001

31 For example, in 2000/01, the 60 per cent of the median (BHC) line was £176 a week (equivalised income); while 50 per cent of the mean (BHC) was £181 a week. If self-employment incomes were excluded the figures were even closer at £174 and 175 per week, respectively. Similarly the AHC figures were £153 a week for 60 per cent of the median and £158 a week for 50 per cent of the mean including self-employment incomes, and £153 and £152 respectively excluding self-employment incomes (Department for Work and Pensions, *Households Below Average Income 2000/01*, p13)

32 For example, the Government's concern in 1997 with the three million children living in poverty was based on such a measure of poverty.

33 For a discussion of the after or before housing costs issues, see P Johnson and S Webb, 'The Treatment of Housing in Official Low Income Statistics', *Journal of the Royal Statistical Society*, Series A, 155, 1992, pp273–290

34 I also quote those figures which include rather than exclude self-employment incomes, following government practice in its *Opportunity for All* indicators. It is also particularly pertinent to include self-employment incomes given the relatively high rates of self-employment among some minority ethnic groups.

35 See for example, B S Rowntree, *Poverty: a study of town life*, Macmillan, 1902; A L Bowley and A R Burnett-Hurst, *Livelihood and Poverty: a study in the economic conditions of working class households in Northampton, Warrington, Stanley and Reading*, G Bell and Sons, 1915

36 J Bradshaw, *Budget Standards for the United Kingdom*, Avebury, 1993; H Parker, *Low Cost but Acceptable: a minimum income standard for the UK*, The Policy Press, 1998; S Middleton, K Ashworth and R Walker, *Family Fortunes: pressures on parents and children in the 1990s*, CPAG, 1994

37 See note 27

38 J Mack and S Lansley, *Poor Britain*, George Allen and Unwin, 1985; D Gordon and C Pantazis, *Breadline Britain in the 1990s*, Ashgate, 1997

39 For example, C T Whelan, R Layte and B Maître, 'Multiple Deprivation and Persistent Poverty in the European Union', *Journal of European Social Policy* 12, May 2002

40 D Gordon, L Adelman, K Ashworth, J Bradshaw, R Levitas, S Middleton, C Pantazis, D Patsios, S Payne, P Townsend and J Williams, *Poverty and Social Exclusion in Britain*, Joseph Rowntree Foundation, 2000

41 Or possibly more than half, if sampling variability is taken into account.

42 This tendency has been illuminatingly explored in the choice versus constraint debate on ethnic minority housing 'preferences'. See for example, P Sarre, 'Choice and Constraint in Ethnic Minority Housing', *Housing Studies* 1, 1986; C Peach and M Byron, 'Council House Sales, Residualisation and Afro-Caribbean Tenants', *Journal of Social Policy* 23, 1994

43 See note 3, p23

44 See note 3, p21

45 For a fuller discussion of the language and definition of social exclusion and its relationship to discussions of intergenerational poverty and the 'cycle of deprivation' see R Levitas, *The Inclusive Society*, Macmillan, 1998. The consequences of poverty are discussed further in Chapter 3.

46 B Barry, *Social Exclusion, Social Isolation and the Distribution of Income*, CasePaper 12, London School of Economics, August 1998

47 M Goodwin, 'Poverty in the City: 'you can raise your voice but who is listening?' in C Philo (ed), *Off the Map: the social geography of poverty in the UK*, CPAG, 1995, discusses the meaning and associations of the 'inner city'. Note also that at one time government indices of local deprivation used proportions of minority groups as one of the measures of deprivation itself, which tended to enhance the allocations to local authorities in London. This has changed with the methodology of the most recent indices. See also the rejection of the concept of social exclusion, both conceptually and for its danger of pathologisation by P Ratcliffe, 'Housing Inequality and 'Race': some critical reflections on the concept of social exclusion', *Ethnic and Racial Studies* 22, 1999, pp1–22

48 See note 27

49 See D Piachaud, *The Cost of a Child*, CPAG, 1979; J Bradshaw, *Budget Standards for the United Kingdom*, Avebury, 1993; H Parker, *Low Cost but Acceptable: a minimum income standard for the UK*, The Policy Press, 1998

50 Office of the Deputy Prime Minister, *Indices of Deprivation 2000*, available at http://www.urban.odpm.gov.uk/research/id2000/index.htm

51 On the issue of the collection of ethnic group benefit information see the discussion, in Chapter 7, of the DWP's Race Equality Scheme consultation

document, *Equality, Opportunity and Independence for All*, 2002

52 L Platt and M Noble, *'Race', Place and Poverty*, Joseph Rowntree Foundation, 1999

53 See, for example, F Falkingham *Take-up of Benefits: a literature review*, Nottingham University, 1986; or P Craig, 'Costs and Benefits: a review of research on take-up of means-tested benefits', *Journal of Social Policy* 20, 1994

54 J Bradshaw, 'Child Poverty Under Labour' in G Fimister (ed), *An End in Sight? Tackling Child Poverty in the UK*, CPAG, 2001, p14

55 See notes 3, 30 and Department of Social Security, *Opportunity for All – One Year On: making a difference*, Second Annual Report, 2000

56 Department for Work and Pensions, *Measuring Child Poverty: a consultation document*, 2002

57 See note 56, p3

58 See note 56, p10

59 For a useful discussion of class definition and measurement in Britain, see K Roberts, *Class in Modern Britain*, Palgrave, 2001

60 D Rose and K O'Reilly, *The ESRC Review of Government Social Classifications*, ONS, 1998; 'The National Statistics Socio-economic Classification' at http://www.statistics.gov.uk/methods_quality/ns_sec/

61 J H Goldthorpe and K Hope, *The Social Grading of Occupations: a new approach and scale*, Clarendon, 1974; R Erickson and J H Goldthorpe, *The Constant Flux : a study of class mobility in industrial societies*, Clarendon, 1992

62 DSS Press Release, 'Family Resources Survey 1995/96', 29 August 1997

63 T Modood, R Berthoud *et al*, *Ethnic Minorities in Britain: diversity and disadvantage*, Policy Studies Institute, 1997

Three

The extent of poverty among minority ethnic groups

This chapter describes the extent of poverty among the different minority ethnic groups, both overall and at different ages. It does this by considering income information, predominantly derived from the *Family Resources Survey*, but supported by findings from other sources. It explores ethnic minorities' experience of poverty in relation to the different measures of poverty outlined in Chapter 2. It also indicates some of the different characteristics associated with different poverty rates, which are explored in more depth in the subsequent chapters.

First, however, it puts what follows into context by considering poverty across the population as a whole.[1] This gives a context to the experience of minority ethnic groups, both in so far as they differ from the overall patterns and in so far as minority groups are concentrated among the poor. It also illustrates the extent to which the experience of poverty is associated with particular characteristics – characteristics which may impact more on some ethnic groups than on others, as is discussed in succeeding chapters.

Poverty among the British population

As discussed in Chapter 2, we can measure those in poverty by counting the number of people with incomes that are below a given fraction of average income; by counting the number of people dependent on means-tested or 'subsistence' benefits; by considering the extent to which incomes are dispersed; by observing the lack of access to 'necessities'; or by assessing the inability to participate effectively in majority life. Despite claims in the 1980s from within government that poverty no longer existed in Britain, that decade saw a sharp increase in those in poverty by any measure.[2] Poverty rates have held much more constant in the 1990s, though there have been differences according to the different measures employed. Here is a brief account of patterns of poverty in the last couple of decades.

Income inequality and those living below fractions of average income

The growth in income inequality over the 1980s and early 1990s was a striking feature of that period.[3] The proportion living below 50 per cent of contemporary mean income after housing costs (AHC) rose from 9 per cent in 1979 to a high of 25 per cent in 1991/92/93 before dropping back slightly in 1995/96.[4] The increased vulnerability to poverty affected children in particular with the proportions below 50 per cent of the mean rising from 1 in 10 to over a third between 1979 and 1995/96.[5] Between the mid-1990s and 2000/01, the proportions living below fractions of average income have stabilised.[6] Thus, despite increasing prosperity and a buoyant economic context with low unemployment there has not been a corresponding drop in the proportions at the bottom of the income distribution.

If average income levels are held constant in real terms the poorest 5 per cent of the income distribution saw a decline in real average income from 1983 to 1993.[7] For this poorest 5 per cent, real incomes were in fact the same in 1991 as they had been in 1966 and 20 per cent lower in 1991 than they had been in 1979. The number of children living in families below half the 1979 mean held constant in real terms increased by 300,000 between 1979 and 1995/96.[8] Since 1994/95 the proportions living below low-income thresholds fixed in real terms have declined, with 15 per cent of individuals and 21 per cent of children living below 60 per cent of the 1994/95 median in 2000/01.[9]

Children thus went from having a risk of poverty comparable to the population as a whole to having a much higher risk of poverty. Children's risk of low income, despite initial increases after 1995/96, has dropped back since 1999 to around 1994/5 levels. By 2000/01 an estimated 3.9 million children were living below 60 per cent of the median: half a million children fewer were living on a low income than in 1996/97 and 200,000 fewer than in 1999/00.[10] The timing of these changes is partly a consequence of the fact that those measures specifically aimed at children, such as the replacement of family credit with working families' tax credit and the increases to child allowances in income support, did not take place till the end of the century.[11]

The levelling off of poverty rates can be attributed in part to measures specifically aimed at reducing child and family poverty, such as increases in amounts of benefit allowed for children and the introduction of tax credits. In addition, since the mid-1990s income growth has been experienced across the whole of the distribution, unlike the preceding 15 years when growth was experienced predominantly at the top of the income distribution.

Figure 3.1

Trend in proportion of individuals and children falling below 60 per cent of median income (AHC), 1979 to 2000/01

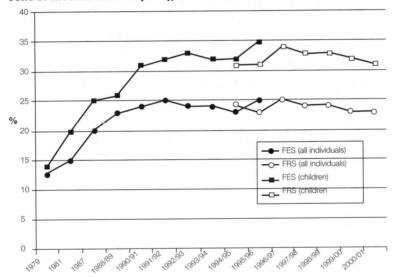

Source: Created from Department for Work and Pensions, *Households Below Average Income 2000/01*, 2002, Tables H1 and H2

The trend, then, illustrated in Figure 3.1, has been one of increasing dispersion of incomes with a large number of people living at current income levels that do not correspond to the greater affluence of the population as a whole. The levels of inequality provide a valuable context for considering the persistent disadvantage of vulnerable sections of the population. Inequality itself is a problem for ethnic minorities to the extent that income distributions are not randomly distributed, but income dispersion differentially affects those from different minority ethnic groups. Thus, increasing inequality indicates increasing polarisation. In addition, the inequality measures themselves can indicate levels of low income and how low income disproportionately affects those with certain characteristics. It can, therefore, tell us about poverty and the relative risk of poverty in the population and provide a point of comparison for the experience of minority ethnic groups considered later in the chapter.

Nevertheless, some would argue, and with good reason, that income inequality and poverty are distinct. A line set at a particular fraction of household income is, to a large extent, an arbitrary definition of poverty and has no necessary connection to what constitutes an income adequate to avoid poverty.[12] Nevertheless, the relational aspect of poverty is well attested:[13] you are poor if you are excluded from general living standards and a fraction of the average does provide a point of reference to the income distribution as a whole. Thus, the proportions of those living below fractions of average income can be taken to be not just an indicator of inequalities with-

Figure 3.2

Proportions of individuals below fractions of average income by family type, 2000/01

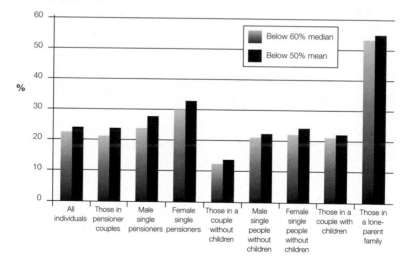

Source: Created from Department for Work and Pensions, *Households Below Average Income 2000/01*, 2002, Table 3.5

in society but also to stand in for an indication of poverty. This has been acknowledged by the Government in its *Opportunity for All* indicators, which use proportions of fractions of contemporary average income and proportions below fractions of average income in the baseline year to establish low income, as discussed above.[14] In addition, this book is explicitly dealing with the relative experience of poverty: not simply the extent of poverty among minority ethnic groups, but also the variation in rates of poverty between ethnic groups. An inequality measure is therefore a valuable way of assessing such variation. There follow, then, the proportions of individuals living at fractions of average income at most recent estimates.

Using the two fractions of average income discussed in Chapter 2 (50 per cent of mean income and 60 per cent of median income) we see that, in 2000/01, 24 per cent of individuals lived at incomes below half the mean (AHC). This is very close to the 23 per cent who were below 60 per cent of the median.[15] The proportions of children living on a low income in 2000/01 were 31 per cent below 60 per cent of the median and 32 per cent below 50 per cent of the mean.[16] Figure 3.2 illustrates the proportions of those living below 60 per cent of the median and 50 per cent of the mean in 2000/01 according to their family characteristics.

Figure 3.2 reveals the higher risk of low income experienced by those in lone-parent families in particular. It also indicates more broadly the extent to which poverty has a gender dimension, and it indicates the fact that pensioners are more likely to be on a low income.

Table 3.1

Percentage of individuals across the income distribution (AHC) by family type, 2000/01

	Poorest fifth	Second fifth	Middle fifth	Fourth fifth	Richest fifth
Children in couple-parent families	19	23	23	19	16
Children in lone-parent families	50	26	14	7	3
All children	**27**	**24**	**21**	**16**	**12**
Working-age adults	**17**	**16**	**19**	**23**	**25**
Pensioner couples	19	27	22	17	15
Single pensioners	21	31	21	15	11
All pensioners	**20**	**29**	**22**	**16**	**13**

Source: Department for Work and Pensions, *Households Below Average Income 2000/01*, 2002, Tables 4.1, 5.2 and 6.1

Table 3.1 shows the proportions of children, of working-age adults and of pensioners living in families with equivalent incomes that place them in different fifths of the income distribution. *Households Below Average Income (HBAI)* includes a division of the income distribution into fifths on the basis of the equivalent incomes of all individuals. Then the proportion with different characteristics that fits the income range of each fifth is calculated. Thus any proportion above 20 per cent constitutes an over-representation in that part of the income distribution and any proportion under 20 per cent represents an under-representation in that part of the income distribution. The table illustrates the impact of family type for children and pensioners, in addition to their overall over-representation at the bottom of the income distribution.

Deprivation

Alternative measures to half average income are consistent with the suggestion of substantial increases in both income inequality and poverty during the 1980s. Mack and Lansley, using their 'democratic' poverty measure, suggested that 14 per cent were living in a state of deprivation in 1983.[17] When they repeated the survey in 1990 they found that poverty had increased to 20 per cent, which parallels the growth in inequality when measured by the relative income measure over this period.[18] It captures in addition, the fact that inequality is not just a function of rising living standards increasing more for those at the top of the distribution, but that it can also indicate a decreasing level of real income at the bottom of the income distribution.

The most recent version of this approach, carried out in 1999 by Gordon and others used a similar methodology of creating consensual definitions of 'necessities'. In addition they developed a separate scale of child necessities. Over 90 per cent of respondents endorsed as necessities such items as 'beds and bedding for all' and 'a damp-free home'. There was also a majority of support for a number of activities or items which enabled some form of social integration, such as 'friends or family round for a meal' (endorsed by 64 per cent). The authors note that 'what is striking is the strength of public acknowledgement that such social activities take their place among the 'necessities' of life'.[19] The authors then ascertained the proportions who could not afford two or more such necessities, and whose incomes did not indicate that they had 'risen out of poverty'. They used a similar approach with children, where necessities were defined as such things as properly fitting shoes, books to read, a school trip every term and a garden to play in. Using this approach they found that around 26 per cent of adults and 18 per cent of children could be estimated to be in poverty.[20] It is worth noting that adults were more likely to suffer deprivation than children; and that as many as 65 per cent of children deemed to be 'income poor' were not lacking the children's necessities. This would seem to suggest that even in low-income families parents can protect their children from deprivation to a certain extent. However, factors that affect their ability to do so will be the severity of the poverty and its persistence. For children living in ethnic minority families who are in poverty, the poverty may well be so extreme that the opportunities to protect them from deprivation are distinctly limited.

A further aspect of deprivation that has gained attention is the issue of area deprivation. Chances of poverty are not evenly distributed, but are geographically clustered. People living in 'deprived areas' are more likely to be poor than those who are not. There is also the fact that the depri-

Figure 3.3

Proportions of individuals below 60 per cent median income by country and region, 2000/01

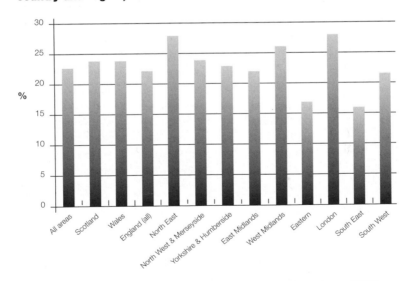

Source: Created from Department for Work and Pensions, *Households Below Average Income 2000/01*, 2002, Table 3.6

vation of an area may itself contribute to or exacerbate an individual's deprivation. The proportions of those living below half average income varies by region, as Figure 3.3 illustrates. We can see, in particular, that there are far higher proportions of individuals on low incomes in London and the North East than in the South East and Eastern areas.

In addition, the Indices of Deprivation, and the Index of Multiple Deprivation derived from it, identify area deprivation in England at a much smaller area of disaggregation. Not only are districts ranked in terms of their overall deprivation but the most deprived wards on a number of char-

Table 3.2

Area deprivation in England: districts and wards with the highest deprivation scores

Ten districts with highest average ward deprivation scores	Ten wards with highest multiple deprivation scores	Ten wards with highest income deprivation scores	Ten wards with highest child poverty deprivation scores
Tower Hamlets	Benchill (Manchester)	Everton (Liverpool)	Bidston (Wirral)
Knowsley	Speke (Liverpool)	Longview (Knowsley)	Princess (Knowsley)
Liverpool	Thorntree (Middlesbrough)	Princess (Knowsley)	Smithdown (Liverpool)
Hackney	Everton (Liverpool)	Vauxhall (Liverpool)	Blackwall (Tower Hamlets)
Newham	Pallister (Middlesbrough)	Grangetown (Redcar and Cleveland)	Beechwood (Middlesbrough)
Manchester	Vauxhall (Liverpool)	Thorntree (Middlesbrough)	Daneshouse (Burnley)
Easington	St. Hilda's (Middlesbrough)	Granby (Liverpool)	West City (Newcastle upon Tyne)
Hartlepool	Princess (Knowsley)	Daneshouse (Burnley)	Vauxhall (Liverpool)
Middlesbrough	Grangetown (Redcar and Cleveland)	Bidston (Wirral)	Noddle Hill (Kingston upon Hull)
Blackburn with Darwen	Granby (Liverpool)	Sparkbrook (Birmingham)	Hardwick (Stockton-on-Tees)

Source: Derived from ODPM, *Indices of Deprivation 2000*

acteristics and on their aggregate can also be identified.[21] Table 3.2 lists those ten English local authorities which, averaging across their wards, experience the highest levels of deprivation overall. In addition it lists those ten wards (and the districts in which they occur) which rank highest for multiple deprivation, for income deprivation and for child poverty.

As Table 3.2 illustrates, the highest overall deprivation is found in some East London local authorities (Hackney, Newham and Tower Hamlets) as well as Merseyside (Liverpool and Knowsley), Lancashire (Manchester and Blackburn with Darwen) and a concentration of districts in the North East (Middlesbrough, Hartlepool and Easington). The most deprived wards predominantly also occur in these general areas, but also reveal that there are severe pockets of deprivation occurring further up (Newcastle upon Tyne) and down (Kingston upon Hull) the North East coast as well as in Birmingham in the West Midlands.

Such awareness of the composite deprivation of small areas provides a means of assessing the social exclusion of *areas*. This can also be extended to the people living in them – both by association and because many of the area measures themselves represent the cumulative experience of the residents, such as unemployment counts, recipients of income support and so on. Residence in such areas may imply a greater vulnerability to deprivation and poverty and its consequences, as well as indicating a more entrenched situation and fewer opportunities for escaping poverty and deprivation.[22] In addition, the experience of living in a deprived area, which may impact on quality of life in a number of ways, could be considered to be an aspect of deprivation itself. Thus, the over-representation of some groups in deprived areas could be taken to have implications for the future experience of the group as well as impacting on its current welfare. The Government's approach to social exclusion and neighbourhood renewal have emphasised the importance of responding to the problems of the most deprived areas, with the implication that areas themselves represent obstacles to equality and opportunity.[23]

Those receiving means-tested benefits

As discussed in Chapter 2, receipt of means-tested benefits has often been associated with low income, and has been taken as a measure of poverty in some studies.[24] While such a definition is not uncontentious, it has nevertheless had a number of valuable applications. What follows is a description of the proportion of the population that is dependent on means-tested benefits and how this varies with different characteristics. Included are the social assistance benefits, income support and income-based jobseeker's allowance, and the housing costs benefits, housing benefit and council tax benefit. While housing benefit and council tax benefit cover a broader income range than income support as they vary to a certain extent with housing costs, still, 90 per cent of recipients of these two benefits fall within the poorer half of the income distribution and 50 per cent of recipients fall within the poorest fifth of the income distribution.[25] Working families' tax credit is another form of means-tested assistance. It is payable to those in work and with children for whom their earnings are insufficient. Like the disabled person's tax credit – a credit payable to those with a disability who tend to be condemned to low income through low earnings and extra costs – working families' tax credit is intended to complement rather than substitute for employment income. These tax credits reach further up the income distribution than their predecessors, though the extent to which working families' tax credit is taken up by eligible families is a cause for concern, an issue discussed further in Chapter 6. Working families' tax credit also interacts with housing and council tax benefits, which can reduce its benefit to those with high rents and at particular points on the income distribution.

According to the *Family Resources Survey 2000/01*, over half of all families[26] (60 per cent) were in receipt of some form of cash benefit, whether means-tested or non-means-tested or both, with just under a quarter of families (21 per cent) in receipt of a means-tested benefit.[27] The most commonly claimed means-tested benefit was council tax benefit, but one in ten families were in receipt of income support or the minimum income guarantee, with a further 3 per cent in receipt of jobseeker's allowance.[28]

Over 90 per cent of families headed by someone of retirement age receive some state retirement pension. At the same time, the value of the basic state pension is below the rate of the minimum income guarantee. In addition, disability, and thus entitlement to disability benefits, is more likely to affect older people. It is, therefore, unsurprising to find benefit receipt concentrated among those of retirement age. While nearly all families headed by someone aged 60 and above receive a non-means-tested benefit, in addition, as Table 3.3 shows, 36 per cent of such families also receive a means-tested benefit, most commonly council tax benefit. Means-tested benefit receipt is lower among working-age adults: the highest rate among those of working age is among families headed by a 25 to 34-year-old, where nearly a fifth are in receipt. For this group, a higher risk of unemployment and of lower wages combines with more limited

Table 3.3

Receipt of means-tested benefits according to family characteristics, 2000/01

Characteristics of family	% of families[29] in receipt of:					
	income support minimum income guarantee	jobseeker's allowance	housing benefit	council tax benefit	working families' tax credit	any income-related benefit
Head or spouse aged 60 or over	17	–	23	33	–	36
Head aged 16-24	6	6	6	6	1	13
Head aged 25-34	10	4	14	15	7	19
Head aged 35-44	10	3	14	15	7	18
Head aged 45-54	7	3	11	13	2	15
Head aged 55-59	9	2	11	15	1	18
Lone-parent families with children	51	1	52	55	24	64
Couple-parent families with children	4	2	7	9	9	10
All families	**10**	**3**	**14**	**17**	**3**	**21**

Source: Adapted from Department for Work and Pensions *Family Resources Survey Great Britain, 2000/01*, 2002, Tables 3.15, 3.16, 3.18 and 3.19

chances to accrue entitlement to national insurance benefits. The low rates of benefit receipt among 16 to 24-year-olds is more due to the fact that this age group is less likely to be eligible for benefits. Table 3.3 also reiterates the very high rates of means-tested benefit receipt among lone parents, with over half of this group receiving income support.

Government figures show that just under 12 per cent of the population of Great Britain lived in families supported by income support in November 2001, including claimants, dependent children and partners.[30] Of the nearly four million claimants, the largest share was made up of older claimants receiving the minimum income guarantee (1.74 million), though many of these will be receiving income support as a top-up to other forms of support. Among working-age claimants, the largest group was those who were disabled (just over a million), followed by around 870,000 lone parents. This latter group, despite the attention focused on it, makes up just over a fifth of income support claimants. Couples with dependants accounted for only 200,000 claimants, but these families account for far more people supported by the benefit, as well as receiving the largest average payments. This is because the number of people in a couple-parent family is typically greater than the number in a lone-parent family. These patterns illustrate not only the large numbers of people who have some experience of claiming social assistance benefits, but also the way that it is demography (and disability) which primarily drives the prevalence of benefit receipt. Thus, there is a very high probability of income support receipt for any lone parent, but as a whole lone parents only make up slightly more than one in five of income support claimants. By contrast, single people, who make up an increasing share of the population, make up over 60 per cent of claimants despite their lower individual risk. As we will see below, not only are different demographic patterns among different ethnic minority groups liable to result in different patterns of benefit receipt, but the risks themselves for particular types of family vary widely.

Of course, with means-tested benefit receipt, we can only measure those who claim successfully. Those who do not claim benefit and those who are wrongly refused do not appear in the figures. Generally, families with children have a high take-up of means-tested benefits with non-take-up being much more of an issue for older people. Issues of take-up in relation to minority ethnic groups are discussed further in Chapter 6.

Those poor for more than a year

As indicated in Chapter 2, poverty as deprivation can often be understood in relation to the duration of poverty: a brief or one-off period of poverty is likely to have less serious implications than poverty which persists over a number of years. By contrast, persistent poverty can be equated with deprivation and possibly with social exclusion as well. Analysis of the *British Household Panel Survey* has revealed both the amount of poverty mobility and the degree of poverty persistence. It shows that in any given year roughly a sixth of the population is poor, but over a four-year period as much as a third of the population can expect to be poor at least once. One in seven can expect to be poor for at least three out of four years, but this risk varies with characteristics such that being a child, pensioner or an individual living in a lone-parent or workless family increases the probability of poverty persistence.[31] Children are at greater risk of poverty persistence than working-age adults. According to the *Opportunity for All* indicators, 16 per cent of children had incomes below 60 per cent of the median for three out of the four years, compared with 7 per cent of work-ing-age adults.[32] These figures rose to 26 per cent and 12 per cent respectively if the higher threshold of 70 per cent of the median was used.

In summary, poverty in Britain is extensive and has increased over recent decades. This has implications for social cohesion, for the extent to which equality of opportunity can be realistically claimed, and even for the extent to which we can continue to conceive of Britain as one nation with common experiences. In addition, poverty does not impact on all groups to the same extent. Poverty can be linked principally both to employment status and to family type (which may itself have implications for employ-ment status). We find, for example, that 90 per cent of those living in a family with an unemployed worker were in the bottom 40 per cent of the income distribution, with three-quarters of those in lone-parent families and over half of those in a family with a disabled adult in the bottom 40 per cent of the income distribution.[33]

Minority group poverty

Despite the awareness of the disadvantaged situation of minority ethnic groups, particularly in areas such as employment, a major advance in describing and understanding the *poverty* of minority ethnic groups was made possible by the *Fourth National Survey of Ethnic Minorities*. Despite some criticisms of the income information in this survey,[34] it was valuable in proving a detailed (and disturbing) picture of the substantial differences in resources available to those of different ethnic groups. In his analysis of the income information from the survey, Berthoud commented that:

> 'The first, and outstanding, finding is the extent of poverty among both Pakistani and Bangladeshi households. We have known from data about employment, earnings and household structure that they must be poor, but the clear measurement has nevertheless been startling. More than four out of five Pakistani and Bangladeshi households fell below a benchmark which affected only a fifth of white non-pensioners. Name any group whose pover-ty causes national concern – pensioners, disabled people, one-parent fam-ilies, the unemployed – Pakistanis and Bangladeshis were poorer.'[35]

This highlights both the extreme nature of the poverty experienced by some minority groups and also the differences *between* the minority

Table 3.4

Household incomes by ethnic group, 1993

Ethnic group	Average equivalent income for households with no earner	Average equivalent income for households with at least one earner
White	£98	£225
Caribbean	£80	£184
Indian and African Asian	£73	£167/£172
Pakistani and Bangladeshi	£57	£94

Source: adapted from R Berthoud 'Incomes and Standards of Living' in T Modood, R Berthoud and others, *Ethnic Minorities in Britain: diversity and disadvantage*, Policy Studies Institute, 1997, Tables 5.3 and 5.4

groups, which can be disguised in simple minority-majority comparisons. Table 3.4 summarises Berthoud's findings, revealing the differences in income between ethnic groups, not only in households without an earner, but even in those with at least one earner.

The two issues highlighted in this table – the excess poverty experienced by *all* minority groups and the differences *between* different groups – are the focus of this chapter in its synthesis of evidence on ethnic minority poverty.

Since the replacement in 1994 of the *Family Expenditure Survey* by the *Family Resources Survey* as the basis of the Government's *HBAI* series, it has been possible to explore differences in income by ethnic group. Although the numbers of those from different minority groups included in the survey remain small in any year, they illustrate clear differences in income, in income distributions and in benefit receipt, as illustrated below. In addition, Berthoud investigated pooled data for 1994/95 and 1995/96, which allowed a greater degree of analysis and differentiation.[36] He compared the incomes of different types of families: working families, non-working families under 60 and pensioner families by ethnic group and found that his groups of Indians, Caribbeans, and Pakistanis and Bangladeshis had less income left over ('available income') than their white counterparts after their 'basic needs' had been taken into account. These basic needs were calculated using a simplified income support scale combined with a housing benefit calculation. On the basis of these calculations he produced the results for the groups considered – shown in Table 3.5.

The point Berthoud made in the figures in Table 3.5, as he did also in his analysis of the *Fourth National Survey of Ethnic Minorities*, is that while

Table 3.5

Median income available after 'basic needs' have been met, by type of family and ethnic group, 1994/95/96, £ per week

	White	Indian	Chinese	Caribbean	African	Pakistani & Bangladeshi
Working families	153	138	134	118	106	52
Pensioners	46	23	na	24	na	21
Non-working families						
under 60	6	2	na	0	-6	0
All families	82	76	88	66	51	27

Source: R Berthoud, *The Incomes of Ethnic Minorities*, Institute for Social and Economic Research, University of Essex, 1998, Table 1.23, p27

na = not calculable due to insufficient numbers

higher levels of poverty among certain groups can sometimes be explained by higher proportions of non-workers (pensioners, most lone parents, unemployed people), a comparison of incomes of those working reveals the insufficiency of such ways of assessing the relative disadvantage of minority groups. The results illustrate an emphatic difference between the incomes of working Pakistani and Bangladeshi families and the incomes of working families from all other groups. But even when not taking account of factors that might 'explain' poverty, there are large differentials in available income by ethnic group. The relative disadvantage of Caribbeans, Africans and, in particular, Pakistanis and Bangladeshis is still evident (see bottom line of Table 3.5). Differences in the relative position of groups when all families are examined compared with working families are driven both by the proportions of pensioners and other non-workers in the different groups and the relative affluence of pensioners within the different groups.

Berthoud's analysis of both the *Fourth National Survey of Ethnic Minorities* and *Family Resources Survey* revealed not only that the position of Bangladeshis and Pakistanis was extreme, but also that even the more 'prosperous' minority groups (Chinese and East African Asians) are still worse off than their white equivalents. The poor economic position of those defined as African is noteworthy, especially given their generally very high level of educational qualifications. These poorer outcomes for even the better-off minority groups are sustained up to the most recent figures, but there are also some differences in the specific experiences of the different groups.

Table 3.6

Percentage of individuals from minority ethnic groups across the income distribution and below 60 per cent of median income (AHC), 1999/00

Ethnic group	Poorest fifth	Second fifth	Middle fifth	Fourth fifth	Richest fifth	Below 60% median
Caribbean	29	20	21	17	13	32
Black African	50	17	8	14	12	52
Indian	31	21	21	18	10	34
Pakistani and Bangladeshi	60	28	4	5	3	67
Other	37	13	17	16	17	38
White	18	20	21	21	21	22
All	20	20	20	20	20	24

Source: Author's analysis of Department for Work and Pensions, *Households Below Average Income 1999/00*, 2002

Table 3.6 shows the distributions of individuals living in households headed by members of different ethnic groups across the income distribution in 1999/00 according to the *HBAI* data. The table also shows the proportions from each group falling below 60 per cent of median income.

From this table we can see that all those minority groups defined in the data are over-represented at the bottom of the income distribution and under-represented at the top. We can also see that higher proportions of all minority groups fall below the half average income poverty line than is the case for the population as a whole. The pattern is least marked for the Indian group and reaches an extreme for the combined Pakistani and Bangladeshi group, where 88 per cent of individuals from these two groups have incomes in the bottom two-fifths of the income distribution, and approaching 70 per cent of them have equivalent incomes below 60 per cent of the median. The black African group also shows substantial disadvantage, though here we have to be slightly cautious about the relatively small sample size on which these proportions are based. Caribbeans are faring rather better than they appeared to have been from Berthoud's earlier analysis. They nevertheless continue to show a skew towards the bottom of the income distribution.

Obviously people are more vulnerable to poverty at different ages, with children and pensioners being over-represented at the lower end of the income distribution, as we saw in Table 3.1. So, are there systematic differences in the demographic and family structure of minority groups that might help explain these patterns? Broadly speaking, households headed by a minority group member are more likely to contain children and less likely to contain pensioners than the average for all households. This pattern is shown in more detail in Table 3.7, and raises the question whether, for example, more Pakistanis and Bangladeshis are poor because more of them are children or whether more children are poor because there is a relatively high proportion from minority groups. The response to this question will suggest particular policy initiatives to correct the imbalance. The former answer would suggest more measures are needed to ensure the welfare of children; the latter answer would imply the need for greater measures to combat minority ethnic group disadvantage.

These questions are taken up further in subsequent chapters. However, as a first step, we can compare the distributions relative to people of the same age. Table 3.8 reports the shares of children falling into different fifths of the income distribution according to their ethnic group. A breakdown for pensioners was not possible due to the small numbers in the survey of pensioners from individual minority groups. As Table 3.8 and Figure 3.4 illustrate, we see that whichever group we are looking at, ethnic minority children experience excess poverty both compared to the rates in the minority group as a whole and compared to children in the population as a whole. Children generally are over-represented at the bottom of the income distribution with over 50 per cent in the bottom two fifths; but in an extraordinary level of concentration, over 90 per cent of Pakistani and Bangladeshi children fall into this part of the income distribution. Looking at the final column of the table, 73 per cent of Pakistani

Table 3.7

Households containing children and pensioners by ethnic group, 2000/01

	Black groups	Indian	Pakistani and Bangladeshi	Other	White	All
% of households with children	39	45	72	38	28	**29**
% of households with a pensioner	13	19	16	15	32	**31**

Source: Adapted from Department for Work and Pensions, *Family Resources Survey Great Britain 2000/01*, Table 2.6

Table 3.8

Percentage of children across the income distribution and below 60 per cent of mean income (AHC) by ethnic group, 1999/00

	Poorest fifth	Second fifth	Middle fifth	Fourth fifth	Richest fifth	Below 60% of median
Caribbean	36	25	20	13	6	40
Black African	61	18	6	11	4	63
Indian	43	23	20	11	4	47
Pakistani and Bangladeshi	65	28	3	3	2	73
Other	45	18	15	10	12	46
White	25	23	22	17	13	29
All children	**28**	**23**	**21**	**16**	**12**	**32**

Source: Author's analysis from Department for Work and Pensions, *Households Below Average Income 1999/00*, 2002

and Bangladeshi children live at income levels 60% of the median. Among other minority groups, over 60 per cent of children are in the poorest two-fifths of the income distribution, with black African children showing very high concentrations of low income. Hence, it is clear that we are not simply seeing the consequences of a greater prevalence of families with children within certain groups translating into higher rates of child poverty, though this still remains a probable contributory factor to the higher rates of poverty.

The excess of low income both among the minority groups as a whole and among children from the minority groups in particular, while consistent with Berthoud's earlier findings, continue to shock through their severity and persistence. We see, therefore, that income inequality and excess poverty are clearly issues for all reported minority groups but are most extreme for those of Pakistani or Bangladeshi origin. The issues raised in the earlier part of the 1990s in relation to excess poverty and differences between minority groups remained pertinent at the turn of the millennium. The consistency in the patterns revealed implies a level of entrenched disadvantage that the passage of time is not mitigating. The extent to which more detailed analysis supports such a pessimistic outlook is considered in Chapters 4 to 6; the issue as to whether we can and should be thinking about 'parallel lives' and, if so, how to approach them is one taken up in the concluding Chapter 7.

Figure 3.4

All individuals and children below 60 per cent of median income by ethnic group, 1999/00

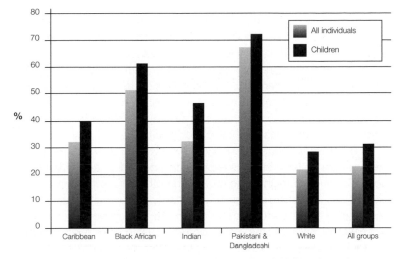

Source: Author's analysis from Department for Work and Pensions, *Households Below Average Income 1999/00*, 2002

Considered next is ethnic minorities' experience in relation to the other indicators of poverty discussed in the previous chapter and outlined for the overall population in the first section of this chapter. I consider critically the amount we know about the differences between groups according to such measures and the implications that arise from the findings in relation to the different perspectives taken.

Deprivation

As discussed in Chapter 2, consensual or democratic studies of deprivation have not provided breakdowns by ethnic group, nor as I argued, do they necessarily constitute the most appropriate method for understanding the deprivation of ethnic minority groups. Nevertheless, there are some sources of information on the experience of deprivation among minority groups.

The *Fourth National Survey of Ethnic Minorities* looked at hardship in relation to money worries, arrears and possession of consumer durables.[37] Obviously, these correlate with income, but, even when income is taken into account, there are distinctive patterns according to ethnicity. Caribbeans, Indians and East African Asians, and, especially, Pakistanis and Bangladeshis were less likely to own consumer durables than even their income levels would suggest, while the Chinese were rather more likely to. This may reflect the relationship between deprivation and longer-term income deficits, as opposed to current income, that was raised in Chapter 2. The ability to build up or replace goods is clearly related not only to current income but also to long-term financial history and prospects. Income uncertainty may also affect decisions about whether to purchase expensive items. Conversely, confidence about future prospects may lead to 'anticipatory' purchases, in the way that higher education students' expenditure tends to outstrip their income.

The findings about arrears and money worries showed a rather different pattern, with Caribbeans experiencing more debt and anxiety than their income levels might indicate and the other ethnic minority groups experiencing less of these. Again, uncertainty rather than actual current income may affect Caribbeans in relation to money worries, and past experience of lower income may have resulted in greater debts. There is substantial evidence (explored in Chapter 5) that many Caribbeans spend an extended period of time in education, which will influence their accumulation of debt, as well as of durables at subsequent stages. And debt itself is likely to induce financial worry. This does not, however, explain the lower rates of arrears and money worries among Indians and African Asians and among Pakistanis and Bangladeshis. Here, however, cultural factors might deserve consideration, such as religious resistance to borrowing money at interest or potential sources of community support, as well as within-family transfers. Cohen and others revealed the importance of informal systems of borrowing and lending in the lives of the Pakistanis interviewed.[38] But they also conveyed the anxiety and reciprocal obligations that went with such structures of informal borrowing and formal gift-giving. The difficulties in obtaining viable sources of credit across Bangladeshi, Pakistani and Caribbean communities have also been identified, and the distinct patterns of credit use analysed.[39] These topics may well repay further exploration.

It may also be that it is *fluctuations* in income rather than continuous low income that is likely to result in arrears and anxiety: this would be supported by the evidence that pensioners are less likely to have durables, but also less likely to report arrears or financial anxiety. Nevertheless, this latter hypothesis could only be properly investigated if more were known about the patterns of income dynamics among minority groups.

Related to this issue of hardship is that of assets and savings. According to figures published in *Social Trends* in 2001, in the population as a whole, 28 per cent had no savings at all, while just a slightly smaller proportion, 24 per cent, had savings of £10,000 or more.[40] However, among black groups, those without savings amount to 54 per cent, with only 3 per cent having £10,000 or more in savings. A comparable picture was found among Pakistanis and Bangladeshis with 60 per cent having no savings and 4 per cent with £10,000 or more. Interestingly, whereas there is a slightly higher proportion of Indians with no savings than in the population at large (30 per cent), this group also has a higher proportion of those with £10,000 or more at 28 per cent. These patterns will be in part related to the age structure of the populations, with older people more likely to have built up assets and savings, although the very oldest are likely to have exhausted their savings. They are also related to the life-time experience of income and poverty, which will impact on the possibilities of building up savings. However, the position of the Indians does not fit with these explanations, since they have both a younger age profile than the population as a whole and they experience higher rates of poverty than the overall population. There would seem to be additional factors that influence the building up of savings among certain groups.

A further factor influencing the ability of some minority group members to accrue assets and to avoid hardship is the extent to which income is sent abroad or contributed to projects or property outside Britain, and the impact of that on the experience of minorities in Britain. Both the *Third* (1982) and *Fourth* (1993) *National Surveys of Ethnic Minorities* showed that substantial amounts were regularly sent 'home' by Caribbeans (well over a third of them sending remittances to other households), with a smaller, but still substantial, proportion of South Asians doing so.[41] Boneham in her study of older people from minority groups in Liverpool found that, despite the fact that her respondents were past retirement age, over a quarter of them sent money or gifts overseas.[42]

An alternative assessment of ethnic minority deprivation can be explored through comparison of housing deprivation. There is substantial evidence that housing quality varies with ethnic group. The *English House Conditions Survey* indicated in the early 1990s that twice as many of those from Asian and black groups than from white groups were living in houses in the worst state of repair.[43] This survey also confirmed findings from the 1991 Census that indicated differences in levels of overcrowding, with nearly one in five Bangladeshis living at a density of more than 1.5 persons a room. The experience of overcrowding among Bangladeshis as well as a consideration of its possible causes has been illustrated in a study of Tower Hamlets.[44] The poor quality or lack of amenity in housing occupied by Pakistanis has also been noted.[45] Summarising the evidence, Bowes and Sim point out that 'either Pakistani households have found great difficulty in accessing good quality accommodation or, alternatively, in improving sub-standard housing with grant assistance.'[46] While tenure itself is not an indication of housing deprivation, the evidence suggests that within tenures minority groups tend to fare worse than their white counterparts. For example, black Caribbeans in local authority housing are more likely to be living in flats or maisonettes than in houses, and those in flats are more likely to be on high floors.[47] Pakistani owner occupation tends to be in the older terraces of inner cities; and Bangladeshis in local authority accommodation have tended to be allocated to – and spatially concentrated in – the least desirable properties.[48] The Chinese, along with the Indians appear to hold a relatively strong housing position,[49] but a substantial segment of the Chinese population also live in non-self-contained flatted accommodation.[50]

Cohen and others illustrated the difficulties of participating in traditional practices for those existing on income support, as well as the lack of what was deemed to be a meaningful life, which stemmed from the pressures of poverty. The isolation and psychological stress is conveyed by Anjum Abbas, a separated mother with two children, who comments: 'I have to cope, with difficulty. But life is nothing, it hasn't been so far and I don't think it will be in the future.'[51]

The same source emphasises the exclusion of children from important social practices, such as religious festivals, through the unavailability of funds for new clothing. The deprivation of children is also treated in a study by Moore.[52] Using the Sample of Anonymised Records from the 1991 Census, he creates with the measures available a fairly minimal deprivation index for children. The rates of deprivation are then analysed according to the ethnic group of the child. From this study, the extreme deprivation of Bangladeshi children is immediately noticeable, with over a quarter (27 per cent) in the most deprived group (compared to 2 per cent overall), and 58 per cent if the top two most deprived groups are taken into account (14 per cent overall). The Bangladeshi children are much more deprived even than Pakistani children who have deprivation rates of 9 per cent in the most deprived category and 34 per cent totalling the top two deprivation categories. In fact, the second most deprived group of children is black African with roughly 14 per cent in the most deprived group and 43 per cent in the top two groups combined. This highlights the particular and peculiarly deprived profile of black Africans, whose characteristics make them closer to Bangladeshis on some measures of deprivation, such as this, but closer to Indians when their educational level is considered. Black Caribbean children also had a high excess of deprivation which was almost identical to the 'black other' proportions, but Indian children experienced less deprivation.

Social exclusion and area deprivation

As discussed above, a key component of social exclusion is the geographical clustering of disadvantage. The concentration of members of minority groups in deprived areas is relevant to their social exclusion in the present and to the persistence of disadvantage into the future. Residential patterns and geographical concentration can be related to patterns of past migration and discriminatory responses in the housing and labour markets. It is thus a demonstration of the outcome of past disadvantage as well as a potential cause of further, future disadvantage.

Concentration in particular types of employment from the earliest period of post-war migration led to specific patterns of residence and high levels of geographical concentration for minority ethnic groups.[53] Such patterns of concentration were exacerbated by discrimination in housing provision, both public and private, and were sustained by restricted employment opportunities and processes of chain migration following the 1962 Commonwealth Immigrants Act. The consequence was an over-representation of minority groups in the least desirable housing and neighbourhoods.[54]

The actual patterns of residence and tenure varied, however, by ethnic group, and tenure itself varied within ethnic groups according to where they were resident. For Indians and Pakistanis, restricted housing opportunities in areas of labour demand meant that the pooling of capital for the purchase of, often dilapidated, inner city houses became an option. Such purchase of undesirable housing in undesirable areas was on occasion supported by favourable local authority mortgages. Owner occupation, rather than representing a positive choice was instead indicative of constraints and resulted in the poor dwelling quality discussed above. Thus a concentration of these groups built up in deprived inner city areas, which had often been, at one stage, marked out for slum clearance. The more highly-skilled and mobile Indian group has subsequently shown a move towards the suburbs, with some indication of a genuine preference for a certain level of owner occupation and middle class Indian concentration, but Pakistanis have remained in relatively deprived geographical concentrations. For Caribbeans, their earlier settlement meant that they were more likely to have fulfilled residence requirements for local authority housing before the building of such housing and resettlement slowed. Options for the pooling of capital also seem to have been less. They thus developed patterns of council housing tenure. However, discriminatory practices within public housing administration or assumptions of 'preferences' tended to leave them in the least desirable parts of the social housing sector, which subsequently became the least desirable for purchase following the introduction of the Right to Buy in 1980. Contrary to the stereotype of a lower cultural preference for owner occupation, Peach and Byron demonstrated that Caribbeans had, if anything, a greater commitment to owning their own homes than their white counterparts. Instead, their continuing over-representation in social housing reflected more limited incomes and the less desirable nature of the council housing they occupied on the introduction and extension of the right to buy, as well as a greater preponderance of family forms, such as lone parents, with lower incomes and less access to capital.[55]

Race relations legislation of the late 1960s and mid 1970s was insufficient to counteract the housing and residential patterns that had become established, particularly when they were reinforced by the decline of manufacturing and processes of deindustrialisation, which further limited the mobility of those already living in the inner cities.[56] As Phillips put it:

> 'The combined forces for minority ethnic clustering produced an early pattern of black concentration, segregation *and* deprivation. This has had long-term repercussions for the pattern of minority ethnic settlement.'[57]

Finally Bangladeshi residence was critically influenced by their relatively late period of migration. Thus, by the time they were occupying council housing it had ceased to be a desirable housing option, as it was in the 1950s, and had become a residual form of tenancy. The processes of immigration, furthermore, tended to result in clustering, particularly in London, an area of extremely high housing cost. For those with limited incomes and/or large families, the now highly residualised social housing sector was often the only option. Thus Bangladeshis show high levels of concentration in some of the poorest areas.

Figure 3.3 showed the relative income inequality across the countries of Great Britain and the regions of England in 2001. The two most deprived regions were London and the North East. London, as Figure 3.5 illustrates, has a composition which shows substantial proportions of minority groups. All minority groups account for 28 per cent of the London population, whereas they account for only 8 per cent of the population of England overall.

Another way of describing this relative concentration is to consider the shares of the different groups which are resident in London. As Figure 3.6 shows, nearly 80 per cent of Britain's black Africans live in London and over half of Britain's Bangladeshis and Caribbeans do, compared with under 10 per cent of the white population of Britain.

On the other hand, the North East has only very small proportions from the minority ethnic groups. If we look to a smaller level of aggregation, following the district and ward breakdowns cited above, we can see that Liverpool and Manchester have high concentrations of minority

Figure 3.5

The ethnic group composition of London, 2001

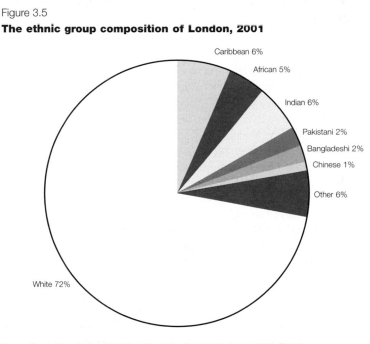

Source: Created from National Statistics, *Population Trends* 105, Autumn 2001, Table 2

Figure 3.6

Proportions of ethnic groups living in London, 2001

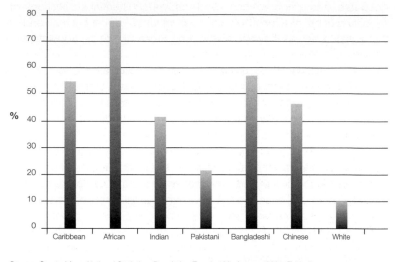

Source: Created from National Statistics, *Population Trends* 105, Autumn 2001, Table 2

groups, as do Tower Hamlets and Newham. Tower Hamlets not only has very high concentrations of Bangladeshis, but Bangladeshis there show the highest concentration of any minority ethnic group at ward and enumeration district level.[58] In addition, the one Birmingham ward that features in the top ten on the income measure in Table 3.2 is Sparkbrook, a ward noted for its relatively large Pakistani concentration.[59] Studies of Birmingham have shown a longstanding identification between those areas with high deprivation and those areas with high proportions of minority ethnic groups.[60] This association between those areas with extreme deprivation and those with high proportions of minority ethnic groups, particularly Pakistani and Bangladeshi groups, was vividly illustrated as persisting or being enhanced in 1998.[61]

Pakistanis, Caribbeans, black Africans and Bangladeshis are thus substantially over-represented in deprived areas, and many, though not all, of the most deprived areas in Britain show substantial concentrations of one or more of these minority groups.

Nevertheless, despite the over-representation in deprived areas, minority group population concentration *on its own* does not necessarily translate into deprivation. It is when the population concentration occurs in deprived areas that it raises concerns about the exclusion of minority groups and the additional impacts of living in a deprived area. Population concentration on its own may be indicative, at least in part and for some groups of choice and the voluntary development of desired communities. This may have positive effects on the experience of those groups as has been argued in relation to the settlement of middle-class Indians in certain areas of outer London.[62] Related to this is the issue of harassment, which for minority ethnic groups can form an additional aspect of area concentration and social exclusion. Racial harassment and what the *Parekh Report* refers to as 'street racism' are both particular aspects of exclusion and deprivation that are suffered by minority ethnic groups and are also likely to occur more in some environments than others.[63] Deprived individuals and individuals in deprived areas are more vulnerable to harassment and racist intimidation. However, there is also the complication that those areas which, while deprived, contain concentrations of particular minority groups may feel safer to members of those groups than other less deprived areas in which minority group members are more isolated.[64]

Further aspects of social exclusion, which were identified in the study by Gordon and others (discussed above), were access to and appropriateness of services and levels of isolation. These aspects of social exclusion may well be ones which are particularly relevant to certain minority groups, and deserve further investigation. However, it was not shown by Gordon and others how far the four areas of exclusion correlate with each other. Until such information becomes available, it will not be possible to ascertain the prevalence of social exclusion as a clustering of the different forms of exclusion, and therefore reveal a point of comparison for minority ethnic groups. While the literature on neighbourhood disadvantage contains discussion of service deprivation and amenity, as well as housing deprivation, this does not capture how service deprivation is experienced at the individual level.

The Social Exclusion Unit treated the issue of minority group exclusion by bringing together information on disadvantage across a range of individual areas, rather than attempting a synthetic picture of minority group exclusion.[65] In so far as it covers the areas critical to what is deemed to be the creation of social exclusion it is the evidence from the book as a whole which informs us about social exclusion among minority groups rather than it being possible to provide single rates or measures for the different groups. In addition, as this discussion has indicated, the extent to which social exclusion is separable from income issues remains debatable. I would argue that the other measures of poverty discussed and the elucidation of their causes that follows in subsequent chapters capture the extent of social exclusion experienced by the different groups.

Benefit receipt

Information on the ethnic group of benefit recipients is not collected by the Department for Work and Pensions. However, it is, again, possible to use the *Family Resources Survey* to get some idea of differences in claiming patterns between ethnic groups. Table 3.9 illustrates the substantial differences between ethnic groups in the proportions of families receiving a means-tested benefit. Thirty-five per cent of Pakistani and Bangladeshi families and 34 per cent of families from black groups are in this position compared with only 21 per cent overall, despite the low numbers of pensioners among these groups. The table also reveals the relatively privileged position of the Indian group on this measure. Looking just at income

Table 3.9

Percentage of families[66] in receipt of means-tested benefits by ethnic group, 2000/01

	All groups	Black groups	Indian	Pakistani & Bangladeshi	Other	White
Income support/ minimum income guarantee	**10**	15	10	20	13	10
Jobseeker's allowance*	**3**	9	2	6	4	3
Housing benefit	**14**	26	8	18	15	13
Council tax benefit	**17**	27	16	29	17	17
Working families' tax credit	**3**	3	3	11	3	3
Any income-related benefit	**21**	**34**	**16**	**35**	**25**	**20**

* This includes the national insurance as well as the means-tested elements; however the national insurance element makes up a small proportion of the benefit.

Source: Adapted from Department for Work and Pensions, *Family Resources Survey Great Britain 2000/01*, 2002, Table 3.17

support and jobseeker's allowance, it shows that 24 per cent of black families and 26 per cent of Pakistani and Bangladeshi families are in receipt of one of these benefits. Despite their high rates of income support and jobseeker's allowance receipt, Pakistani and Bangladeshi families also show the highest numbers in receipt of working families' tax credit. While this is partly a reflection of the large proportions of families with children, it also illustrates that they suffer not only from worklessness, but additionally from low pay when in work.

Further information about benefit receipt can be provided by local authorities, as they occasionally collect information about the ethnicity of recipients of locally administered benefits. In such cases, information can be adduced about the ethnic profile of both housing benefit and council tax benefit receipt at the local authority level and also about those income support or income-based jobseeker's allowance recipients who are also in receipt of housing and/or council tax benefit. In Birmingham in 1998 the substantial over-representation of Pakistanis and Bangladeshis and, to a lesser extent, Caribbeans, on means-tested benefits was demonstrated through analysis of such data.[67] Platt and Noble's study showed that approximately 45 per cent of Bangladeshis were in receipt of either housing benefit or council tax benefit *and* income support, a fraction that increased to around well over half of those living in Bangladeshi families supported by housing benefit or council tax benefit with or without income support. The corresponding figures for Caribbeans were 20 per cent on income support, and 30 per cent when all those on housing or council tax benefit were counted. And for Pakistanis the rates were over 30 per cent if just those on income support were counted, but over 40 per cent if all those supported by housing benefit and/or council tax benefit were considered. These compare with rates in the white population of 14 per cent on income support as well as housing or council tax benefits, and 20 per cent when all those on housing benefit were considered. This study revealed the extent to which the commonly used aggregate Pakistani and Bangladeshi category tends partially to disguise the extreme situation of Bangladeshis. Though Bangladeshis are usually found with Pakistanis at the bottom end of the income distribution, the differences between the actual poverty rates experienced by the two groups can be as great as, or greater than, the differences between the Pakistani experience and that of other minority groups. This distinction between the two groups, with the Bangladeshis in an extreme position, is found whenever the two groups are distinguished.

Those poor over time

As discussed, the experience of poverty is increasingly seen as critically affected by the length of time spent in poverty: that is, its persistence or recurrence. This aspect of poverty, persistence on low income, would also seem to vary by ethnic group. Labour market studies, for example, show that length of time in unemployment varies by ethnic group, but there is little direct evidence on *poverty* dynamics among Britain's minority ethnic groups.

My work on poverty persistence among children using benefit receipt as an indicator suggests that, somewhat paradoxically, among those children who are ever poor, poverty *persistence* is greatest among children in white families, but it is also children from white families who are also most likely to avoid poverty in the first place.[68] Children from Bangladeshi and Pakistani families who are ever poor are more likely to experience a pattern of moves into and out of benefit, and their lower rates of poverty persistence can be explained by family type (ie, more couple parents rather than lone parents). Given the higher prevalence of poverty among these groups in the first place, this implies that the majority, in particular of Bangladeshi children, are living on the margins of poverty. Even when they move out of it they move neither very far nor for very long. Interestingly, despite the high rates of lone parenthood among Caribbean parents they still have lower poverty persistence than other groups. This suggests that the experience of lone parenthood is rather different among Caribbeans than within the population as a whole, an issue discussed further in Chapters 4 and 5.

The consequences of poverty

Poverty is, as we know, associated with poorer outcomes in many areas of life. Poverty means not only a restricted, difficult and often lonely existence of material hardship and social isolation, it has potentially damaging consequences in relation to health, housing, education, experience and fear of crime, and experience of discrimination.[69] In fact, some descriptions of poverty see such consequences and associations as defining it. For example, in The Copenhagen Declaration of 1995 the UN described poverty in the following terms:

> 'Poverty has various manifestations, including lack of income and productive resources sufficient to ensure sustainable livelihoods; hunger and mal-

nutrition; ill health; limited or lack of access to education and other basic services; increased morbidity and mortality from illness; homelessness and inadequate housing; unsafe environments; and social discrimination and exclusion. It is also characterised by a lack of participation in decision making and in civil, social and cultural life. It occurs in all countries...

Furthermore, poverty in its various forms represents a barrier to communication and access to services, as well as a major health risk...'[70]

Poverty in Britain has been associated with poorer health outcomes, including greater levels of sickness and disability and decreases in longevity.[71] The psychological stress caused by poverty is also well attested.[72] Poverty can reduce the ability to participate in political and social institutions, resulting in social exclusion.[73] Poverty can limit access to services and can mean living in unhealthy, unpleasant or stressful surroundings.[74] Poverty, for those growing up in it, can affect not only current quality of life, but also the future: childhood experiences and effects on educational achievement and opportunities can have long-term consequences, as will limited opportunities for geographical mobility.[75] While it is not within the scope of this book to reflect on these associations in any detail, it is important to reflect that in speaking about poverty or low income experience we are talking not simply about the struggles of getting by day to day on insufficient income, but also about the potentially damaging consequences for an individual's future and for future generations.

Thus there is a danger that poverty in one generation will result in poverty in the next. The high rates of poverty among children and among children from certain ethnic minority groups in particular make this a grave cause for concern for the future. The implications of this in relation to minority ethnic groups' poverty are that those belonging to certain groups will become increasingly likely to be separated from the majority experience, that disadvantage will be reinforced over time, and that the association between ethnicity and disadvantage among certain groups will be enhanced. Such entrenched consequences become increasingly difficult to rectify through good practice recommendations or through race relations legislation, which tends to operate at an individual level. Instead, there is a need in addition for structural change and more holistic solutions to the issues of ethnic minority poverty. These issues are picked up on in Chapter 7.

First, Chapters 4 to 6 explore in more detail the factors that contribute to the patterns of minority ethnic groups' poverty. They explore the reasons for the different experience of poverty according to ethnic group. They consider the extent to which the patterns and associations revealed can be accounted for by family type, discrimination, employment experience and social security support; and to what extent such factors remain insufficient in fully explaining minority groups' poverty rates.

Notes

1 See M Howard, A Garnham, G Fimister and J Veit-Wilson, *Poverty: the facts*, CPAG, 2001 for a fuller discussion of the extent and nature of poverty in Britain as summarised here.

2 See C Oppenheim and L Harker, *Poverty: the facts*, CPAG, 1996, pp8-9 for politicians' claims about the non-existence of poverty in the 1980s.

3 A Goodman, P Johnson and S Webb, *Inequality in the UK*, OUP, 1997; J Hills, *Inquiry into Income and Wealth*, Joseph Rowntree Foundation, 1995

4 Department for Work and Pensions, *Households Below Average Income 2000/01*, DWP, 2002, Table H1, p197. These estimates are derived from the *Family Expenditure Survey* which was the source of income information for the period. They therefore apply to the United Kingdom, rather than Great Britain. The comparable figures for those below 60 per cent of the median show an increase from 13 per cent in 1979 to 25 per cent by 1995/96.

5 See note 4, Table H2 p199. The comparable figures for children below 60 per cent of the median show an increase from 14 per cent of children in 1979 to 35 per cent in 1995/96.

6 See note 4, p15

7 See note 2

8 J Bradshaw, 'Child Poverty under Labour' in G Fimister (ed), *An End in Sight? Tackling child poverty in the UK*, CPAG, 2001, p10

9 See note 4

10 See note 4, Table J3, p234

11 See D Piachaud and H Sutherland, 'Child Poverty in Britain and the New Labour Government', *Journal of Social Policy*, 27, 2001, and G Fimister (ed), *An End in Sight? Tackling child poverty in the UK*, CPAG, 2001, for discussions of child poverty reduction policies under the first term of the current Labour administration.

12 See note 1, p17 and also J Veit-Wilson, 'Horses for Discourses: poverty, purpose and closure in minimum income standards policy' in D Gordon and P Townsend (eds), *Breadline Europe: the measurement of poverty*, The Policy Press, 2000

13 See for example, Peter Townsend's influential formulation of this point in *Poverty in the United Kingdom: a survey of household resources and standards of*

living, Penguin, 1979. See also David Piachaud's discussion in his article, 'Research Note: Poverty in Britain 1899-1983', *Journal of Social Policy* 17, 1988

14 Department for Work and Pensions, *Opportunity for All – Making Progress*, Cm 5260, September 2001, pp176-178, 204-206

15 See note 4, Table 3.5, p33

16 See note 4, Table 4.5, p63

17 J Mack and S Lansley, *Poor Britain*, Allen and Unwin, 1985

18 D Gordon and C Pantazis, *Breadline Britain in the 1990s*, Ashgate, 1997

19 D Gordon, L Adelman, K Ashworth, J Bradshaw, R Levitas, S Middleton, C Pantazis, D Patsios, S Payne, P Townsend and J Williams, *Poverty and Social Exclusion in Britain*, Joseph Rowntree Foundation, 2000, p16

20 See note 19, p19

21 Office of the Deputy Prime Minister, *Indices of Deprivation 2000*, at http://www.urban.odpm.gov.uk/research/id2000/index.htm

22 N Buck, 'Identifying Neighbourhood Effects on Social Exclusion', *Urban Studies* 39, 2001

23 See the aims and research programme of the Social Exclusion Unit and the Neighbourhood Renewal Unit in the Office of the Deputy Prime Minister at http://www.socialexclusionunit.gov.uk/ and http://www.neighbourhood.gov.uk/

24 M Noble, S Y Cheung and G Smith, 'Origins and Destinations: social security claimant dynamics', *Journal of Social Policy* 27, 1998; L Platt and M Noble, *'Race', Place and Poverty*, Joseph Rowntree Foundation, 1999; L Platt, 'Ethnicity and Inequality: British children's experience of means-tested benefits', *Journal of Comparative Family Studies*, forthcoming 2003

25 See note 4, Table G. See note 24 for justifications of the use of housing and council tax benefits as low income measures.

26 The term 'families' is here substituted for 'benefit unit' for simplicity. It refers, therefore, (as it does in the tables) to the immediate family unit of the individual with her/his partner (if any) and dependent children (if any): a unit which is termed in the *Family Resources Survey* the 'benefit unit'.

27 R Walker, *The Making of a Welfare Class*, The Policy Press, 2000, provides a discussion of the extension of benefit payment across the population in his book.

28 While entitlement to jobseeker's allowance can be either on the basis of contri- butions or via the means test, the majority of recipients (80 per cent at January 2002 figures) are entitled via the means test.

29 See note 26

30 Department for Work and Pensions, *Income Support Quarterly Statistical Enquiry*, November 2001, Analytical Services Division, 2001

31 S P Jenkins and J A Rigg, *The Dynamics of Poverty in Britain*, Department for Work and Pensions Research Report 157, 2001

32 See note 14, pp178, 206

33 See note 4, Tables 3.1 and 3.2, pp21 and 23

34 See for example, R Moore, 'Material Deprivation Amongst Ethnic Minority and White Children: the evidence of the Sample of Anonymised Records', in J Bradshaw and R Sainsbury (eds), *Experiencing Poverty*, Ashgate, 2000

35 R Berthoud, 'Incomes and Standards of Living' in T Modood, R Berthoud *et al*, *Ethnic Minorities in Britain: diversity and disadvantage*, Policy Studies Institute, 1997, p180

36 R Berthoud, *The Incomes of Ethnic Minorities*

37 See note 35

38 R Cohen, J Coxall, G Craig and A Sadiq-Sangster, *Hardship Britain: being poor in the 1990s*, CPAG, 1992

39 A Herbert and E Kempson, *Credit Use and Ethnic Minorities*, Policy Studies Institute, 1995

40 Office for National Statistics, *Social Trends 31*, ONS, 2001, p110

41 See note 35

42 M Boneham, 'Shortchanging Black and Minority Ethnic Elders' in J Bradshaw and R Sainsbury (eds), *Experiencing Poverty*, Ashgate, 2000

43 P Ratcliffe, ''Race', Ethnicity and Housing Differentials in Britain' in V Karn, *Ethnicity in the 1991 Census: Volume four: employment, education and housing among the ethnic minority populations of Britain*, ONS, 1997, pp141-142

44 E Kempson, *Overcrowding in Bangladeshi Households: a case study of Tower Hamlets*, Policy Studies Institute, 1999

45 R Ballard, 'The Pakistanis: stability and introspection' in C Peach (ed), *Ethnicity in the 1991 Census: Volume two: the ethnic minority populations of Great Britain*, HMSO, 1996; D Phillips, 'Black Minority Ethnic Concentration, Segregation and Dispersal in Britain', *Urban Studies* 35 (10), 1998, pp1681-1702

46 A Bowes and D Sim, 'Patterns of Residential Settlement among Black and Minority Ethnic Groups' in P Somerville and A Steele *'Race', Housing and Social Exclusion*, Jessica Kingsley, 2002, p52

47 C Peach and M Byron, 'Council House Sales, Residualisation and Afro-Caribbean Tenants', *Journal of Social Policy* 23, 1994

48 See note 43

49 D Phillips, 'The Housing Position of Ethnic Minority Group Home Owners' in V Karn (ed), *Ethnicity in the 1991 Census: Volume four: employment, education and housing among the minority ethnic group populations of Britain*, ONS, 1997

50 See note 43

51 See note 38, p28

52 See note 34

53 Immigration histories are amplified in Chapter 5.

54 J Rex and R Moore, *Race, Community and Conflict: a study of Sparkbrook*, Oxford University Press, 1967; J Henderson and V Karn, *Race, Class and State Housing: inequality and the allocation of public housing in Britain*, Gower, 1987

55 See note 47

56 V Karn, J Kemeny and P Williams, *Home Ownership in the Inner City: salvation or despair?* Gower, 1985

57 D Phillips, 'Black Minority Ethnic Concentration, Segregation and Dispersal in Britain', *Urban Studies* 25 (10), 1998, p1683

58 C Peach and D Rossiter, 'Level and Nature of Spatial Concentration and Segregation of Minority Ethnic Populations in Great Britain, 1991' in P Ratcliffe (ed), *Ethnicity in the 1991 Census: Volume three: social geography and ethnicity in Britain: geographical spread, spatial concentration and internal migration*, ONS, 1996

59 See chapters in C Peach (ed), *Ethnicity in the 1991 Census: Volume two: the ethnic minority populations of Great Britain*, HMSO, 1996, for further discussion of the geographical concentration and dispersion of the groups defined in the 1991 Census.

60 See for example, J Rex and R Moore, *Race, Community and Conflict: a study of Sparkbrook*, Oxford University Press, 1967; P Ratcliffe, *Racism and Reaction: a profile of Handsworth*, Routledge and Kegan Paul, 1981

61 L Platt and M Noble, *'Race', Place and Poverty*, Joseph Rowntree Foundation, 1999

62 R Dorsett, *Ethnic Minorities in the Inner City*, The Policy Press, 1998

63 B Parekh, *The Future of Multi-Ethnic Britain* (The Parekh Report), Profile Books, 2000, pp57-58

64 See note 46

65 Cabinet Office, *Minority Ethnic Issues in Social Exclusion and Neighbourhood Renewal: a guide to the work of the Social Exclusion Unit and the policy action teams so far*, June 2000

66 See note 26

67 See note 61, p21

68 L Platt, 'Ethnicity and Inequality: British children's experience of means-tested benefits', *Journal of Comparative Family Studies*, forthcoming 2003

69 For a summary of some of these effects, see note 1, pp105-128

70 Quoted in D Gordon, 'Measuring Absolute and Overall Poverty', in D Gordon and P Townsend (eds), *Breadline Europe: the measurement of poverty*, The Policy Press, 2000, pp49-50

71 Department of Health, *Inequalities in Health* (The Acheson Report), The Stationary Office, 1998

72 L Rainford *et al*, *Health in England 1998: investigating the links between social inequalities and health*, ONS, 2000

73 See note 19. See also, T Burchardt, 'Social Exclusion: concepts and evidence' in D Gordon and P Townsend (eds), *Breadline Europe: the measurement of poverty*, The Policy Press, 2000

74 E Kempson, *Life on a Low Income*, Joseph Rowntree Foundation, 1996

75 J Ermisch, M Francesconi and D Pevalin, *Outcomes for Children of Poverty*, DWP Research Report 158, 2001; S Machin, 'Childhood Disadvantage and Intergenerational Transmission of Economic Status', in A B Atkinson and J Hills, *Exclusion, Employment and Opportunity*, CASE, 1998

Four

Explaining ethnic minority poverty: family structure and cultural patterns

How do we explain the patterns of poverty among minority ethnic groups? There are two broad sets of explanation. The first of these is associated with factors that might be internal to the groups: demographic structure, large or lone-parent families and low economic activity rates among women from some groups. This set of explanations emphasises the distinctiveness of minority groups, their lifestyle and family choices, and what might be termed cultural factors, and are discussed in this chapter.

The other set of explanations focuses on the relationship between minority groups and the labour market, taking account of: levels of education and qualification; the impact of labour market discrimination; patterns of immigration and settlement; and concentration in certain types of occupation, or in unemployment; as well as the lifecourse impacts of such factors. Such explanations focus on the structural causes of poverty and emphasise constraints within the labour market, which operate to limit ethnic minorities' opportunities to engage in economic activity on a par with the overall population. Obviously the structural and the cultural can often not be neatly separated; 'structural' accounts will often have to take account of demographic factors, such as considering the different proportions of young men in different groups and the higher unemployment risk of young men when exploring differences in unemployment. Structural explanations, and their intersection with cultural ones, are considered in Chapters 5 and 6.

While the two types of explanation are neither mutually exclusive nor sufficient on their own to explain patterns of poverty, they do bring different angles to the question of ethnic minority poverty and, therefore, the sorts of policy which are implied. Thus, demographic and cultural accounts suggest either that patterns will change over time with a process of adjustment to national patterns and norms (with half of minority group members now born in Britain),[1] or that policies should be developed which focus specifically on minority groups and their characteristics. Structural accounts, on the other hand, imply policies directed at employment and educational structures, rather than at the minority groups themselves. This is a distinction worth bearing in mind when policies are considered in Chapter 7, as their assumed impact will depend on the emphasis given to one or other of these explanatory perspectives.

Demographic profile

Owen's analysis of the 1991 Census provided a detailed account of the size and structure of the different minority groups in the population and their growth up to 1991.[2] *Population Trends* for Autumn 2001 provided

Table 4.1

The ethnic group populations of Great Britain, 1991-2000

	1991	1991	2000	2000	% change
	Number	%*	Number**	%	1991-2000
Total	54,888,844	100	57,057,000	100	+4
White	51,873,794	94.5	53,004,000	92.9	+2
Black Caribbean and Black other (+ black mixed)	678,365	1.2	834,000	1.5	+23
Black African	212,362	0.4	440,000	0.8	+101
Indian	840,255	1.5	984,000	1.7	+17
Pakistani	476,555	0.9	675,000	1.2	+42
Bangladeshi	162,835	0.3	257,000	0.4	+58
Chinese	156,938	0.3	149,000	0.3	–5
Other Asian	197,534	0.4	N/A	N/A	–
Other Asian (non-mixed)	N/A	–	242,000	0.4	–
Other***	290,206	0.5	458,000	0.8	+58
All minorities	3,015,051	5.5	4,039,000	7.1	+34

* Figures subject to rounding

** Grossed up from estimates

*** Not directly comparable 1991 group and later estimates.

Sources: Adapted from D Owen, 'Size, Structure and Growth of the Ethnic Minority Populations' in D Coleman and J Salt, *Ethnicity in the 1991 Census: Volume one: demographic characteristics of the ethnic minority populations*, HMSO, 1996; and from ONS, *Population Trends 105*, Autumn 2001, The Stationary Office, Table 1

up-to-date estimates from the *Labour Force Survey* according to the most recent classification, which incorporates the 'mixed' categories established for the 2001 Census.[3] Soon (from early 2003 onwards), ethnic group results from the 2001 Census will themselves become available to correct recent estimates and form the basis of future ones. The counts from the 1991 Census and the estimates for 2000 are shown in Table 4.1. This both illustrates demographic trends and highlights the difficulties posed by changing classifications of groups, as not all the categories are directly comparable.[4]

Figure 4.1 illustrates the growth of the minority group populations over the ten-year period estimated at an increase of one million persons across all the population.

This growth, which has occurred for all the classified minority groups with the exception of the Chinese, is unsurprising in view of the

Figure 4.1

Minority group populations, 1991-2000

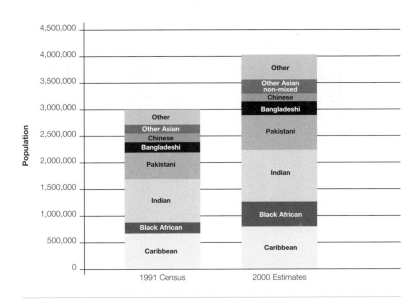

Sources: Derived from D Owen, 'Size, Structure and Growth of the Ethnic Minority Populations' in D Coleman and J Salt (eds), *Ethnicity in the 1991 Census: Volume one: demographic characteristics of the ethnic minority populations*, HMSO, 1996; A Scott, D Pearce and P Goldblatt, 'The Sizes and Characteristics of the Minority Ethnic Populations of Great Britain – latest estimates', *Population Trends* 105, National Statistics, Autumn 2001

minorities' more youthful demographic profile when compared with the population as a whole.

As Table 4.1 illustrates, the biggest proportional population increases between 1991 and 2000 are estimated to be among black Africans, with a doubling of the population. Large increases are also found among the Bangladeshi and Pakistani groups, with the Bangladeshis showing an increase of nearly three-fifths and the Pakistani group estimated to increase by over two-fifths. These increases are driven primarily by fertility and the youthful demographic profile of these groups. The growth in the 'other' groups reflects new patterns of migration over the last decade or so, with primary immigration to Britain now being formed almost entirely of those seeking asylum.

As far as age is concerned, as I have indicated, the minority ethnic groups have a younger demographic profile than the population as a whole, whose profile is heavily influenced by the white population. Figure 4.2 illustrates the distributions of different 15-year age bands across the classified ethnic groups in Britain in 1991.

Figure 4.2

Age profiles of ethnic groups, 1991

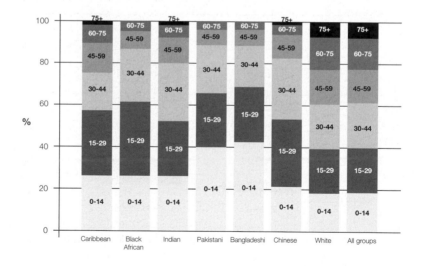

Source: Derived from T Warnes, 'The Age Structure and Ageing of the Ethnic Groups' in D Coleman and J Salt (eds), *Ethnicity in the 1991 Census: Volume one: demographic characteristics of the ethnic minority populations*, HMSO, 1996, Table 6.1

Children

Figure 4.2 shows how children made up a much higher proportion of all the minority groups, with the exception of the Chinese, than they did in the population as a whole. Young adults also made up a substantial share; there were very few of the oldest age group in any of the minority group populations.

The youthful age profile of some groups has implications for poverty, in that families bringing up children have fewer resources than those of working age without children, and children themselves have a higher risk of poverty than the population as a whole. Family size may have some part to play in the differences in poverty between groups, as there are fewer Chinese children relative to adults compared to national profile and a similar number of Indian children – and these are the two minority groups that are most protected against poverty. Therefore, the proportions of children in the different groups is a relevant issue relating to their current poverty; but patterns of fertility are also an important consideration when reflecting on policy for the future.

Estimates for 1997-99, illustrated in Figure 4.3, show that the proportions of children would seem to be declining in the Pakistani and Bangladeshi groups, though they still remain high. The median age for the Bangladeshi group was 18, that is, half those belonging to the Bangladeshi group were under 18, compared with 36 in the population as a whole. On the other hand, the highest proportions of children are found in the new mixed categories, as illustrated in Figure 4.3 by the inclusion of the 'black mixed' estimates. The median age for those in the 'black mixed' and 'other mixed' groups was 11 and 12 respectively. This reflects the extent to which children are now being born to partnerships of mixed ethnicity: in one study, around half of 'Caribbean' children living with both parents had one white parent.[5] It also indicates that this is a trend, unsurprisingly, more among the younger generations than the older ones.

However, it is not clear what the poverty implications are. Insofar as they constitute a minority ethnicity, these mixed ethnicity children are liable to discrimination and to any other disadvantages associated with their ethnicity, which will only become clear once we understand more about the composition of this category. On the other hand, insofar as they constitute a risk of poverty for their parents, it is not clear whose 'risk' they should be seen as. The poverty of the children themselves might also be affected by the risks associated with one parent more than the other, that is, by the extent to which the parent who is the main earner is from a group that has a higher risk of low income.[6] On the other hand, insofar as their very existence is evidence of changing patterns of partnership and family formation, they indicate some of the limitations of demography in accounting for different outcomes.

Figure 4.3

Estimated age profiles of ethnic groups, 1997-99

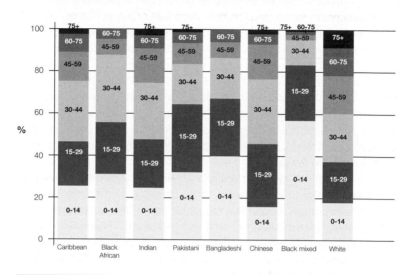

Source: Derived from A Scott, D Pearce and P Goldblatt, 'The Sizes and Characteristics of the Minority Ethnic Populations of Great Britain: latest estimates', *Population Trends* 105, Autumn 2001, Table 3

Older people

Older people are also associated with a higher risk of poverty. However, the proportion of older people is much lower in the minority groups. Nevertheless, although minority group older people make up a smaller share of the relevant populations, older people in minority groups are particularly vulnerable to poverty.[7] There are a number of reasons for this. Because the majority of those from minority ethnic groups who are currently of retirement age will not have spent their full working life in Britain, their contributions record, and therefore their pension entitlement, is likely to have been affected.[8] Extended visits to their home country may also have an impact on contributions. Disadvantage in the labour market during their working years will have prevented the accrual of assets and, often, access to occupational pensions. The habit of sending remittances overseas, more common among those who were born abroad, may have further impinged on available income during the working years and reduced options for putting anything aside or for avoiding material deprivation, a deprivation which will be felt more keenly in old age. Moreover, Boneham's study of 418 older people in Liverpool found that the commitment to sending remittances to the country of origin continued beyond retirement age: 26 per cent of her sample dispatched money or parcels overseas, adding to the pressures on already low incomes.[9] At the same time, assumptions by service providers about extended kin networks can result in unmet need and the failure to provide appropriate community care support.[10] Furthermore, rather than being indicative of protection of older people against poverty, the prevalence of households containing multiple generations may instead be indicative of poverty within the group: as Boneham puts it, 'a situation of group interdependence in a situation of adversity'.[11] There may also be a contributing factor to co-residence stemming from immigration rules about liability to maintain in cases of family reunification, where elderly parents from abroad join their children.

The poverty of currently older people from minority ethnic groups is, then, an issue of concern and one which demands greater attention. Moreover, given the levels of poverty among current working-age adults from certain minority groups, particularly Pakistanis and Bangladeshis, there is clearly an issue for the future when those who have experienced poverty in adulthood reach pension age.

Different family forms: large families and lone-parent families

Related to the issue of age-sex structure is that of the particular family forms that some groups have adopted. Large families and lone-parent families are more likely to be in poverty than other families. To the extent that minority groups show over-representations of these two types of family form, they are more likely to be in poverty.

Lone-parent families have shown a steady increase in Britain over the past few decades, with Britain having one of the highest rates of lone-parent families in Europe. Around one in five families with children is a lone-parent family. The majority of these lone parents are divorced and separated women (and a very small number of men). Increasingly, however, such families are headed by a single, never-married women. While lone parenthood is associated with greater risk of poverty in whichever country it occurs, this is particularly the case in Britain, where it has tended to be associated with non-employment and income support receipt.

Half of Caribbean mothers are single and never married. While this does not necessarily mean that they are without support from the child(ren)'s father, it does, nevertheless, increase their probability of poverty. On the other hand, Caribbean lone mothers are more likely to be working than other lone parents. So, while the overall high numbers of lone parents translates into higher poverty risks for the group, among all lone parents Caribbeans are less likely to be poor. However, they may well be living on the margins of poverty, not only as a result of their family status but also as a result of that interacting with labour market disadvantage.[12] Measures to support lone parents in or into work may, therefore, be particularly beneficial for Caribbean lone parents and may counteract some of the poverty consequent on the high prevalence of this family form.

While the high prevalence of Caribbean lone mothers is often taken to be a cultural issue relating to trends or patterns in the Caribbean countries, the much higher rates among Caribbeans in this country suggest rather more complex factors at work. Caribbeans may be ahead of other groups in rejecting traditional family forms and adhering to more individualistic choices and alternative patterns of family life, in which wider kin and 'visiting' fathers may play a role. There may also be also be issues of the availability of suitable partners; and the fact that educational level and lone parenthood are inversely related may support this interpretation. In this interpretation, lone parenthood for mothers may be a more viable option than parenthood within a partnership.[13] This also suggests that to read 'cultural' explanations from systematic differences without paying attention to the role of structural constraints in sustaining such patterns is inappropriate.

Just as the number of lone-parent families has increased over the last few decades, the number of large families has decreased. Large families are becoming less prevalent in Britain, but where they do occur they are also related to higher risk of poverty. This is in contrast to some European countries where family benefits are structured so as to be more generous to larger families. While Caribbean families show a greater prevalence of lone-parent families than the average, Pakistani and Bangladeshi families have a greater predominance of larger families, which also tends to lead to higher levels of poverty.[14]

Total period fertility rates – that is, the amount of children that a women could be expected to produce during her child-bearing years – have declined from 2.77 in 1961 to 1.66 in 1999. As Berthoud points out: 'Large families were a significant area of British social policy interest until the 1970s...but are so rare now that they have virtually disappeared from the research agenda'.[15] While the reduction in family size is a general trend, not only in Britain but also across Europe, it disguises the variation that exists across different ethnic groups. In the early 1990s, 43 per cent of Bangladeshi and 33 per cent of Pakistani families contained four or more children, compared with 7 per cent of Caribbean families, 4 per cent of white families and 3 per cent of African Asian families, as Figure 4.4 shows.

If only those families which had completed their childbearing were considered, the proportion of Pakistani and Bangladeshi families with four or more children rose to over half. Large families are harder to support on the basis of earnings alone, making poverty in work or poverty through means-tested benefit dependence more likely. While it is poverty in work that is most striking, as we saw in Chapter 3, it has also been shown that

Figure 4.4

Number of children per family by ethnic group, 1993

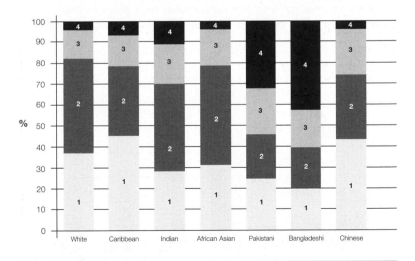

Source: Adapted from R Berthoud and S Beishon 'People, Families and Households' in T Modood, R Berthoud *et al*, *Ethnic Minorities in Britain: diversity and disadvantage*, Table 2.12

Figure 4.5

Households with children by number of children, 2000/01

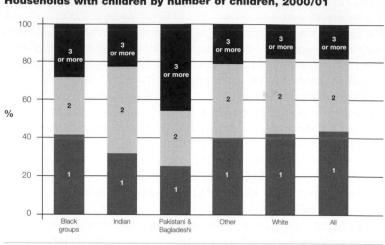

Source: Derived from Department for Work and Pensions, *Family Resources Survey 2000/01*, Table 2.6

Figure 4.6

Households with children and households with three or more children as a share of all households by ethnic group, 2000/01

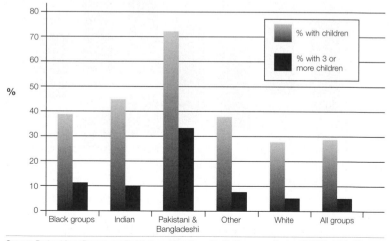

Source: Derived from Department for Work and Pensions, *Family Resources Survey 2000/01*, Table 2.6

for those living on means-tested benefits larger families are also worse off than smaller ones, with extremes being experienced by the large Bangladeshi families on means-tested benefits.[16] Bangladeshi and Pakistani family size may decline over time as demographic patterns shift, though the evidence for 2000/01 from the *Family Resources Survey* still shows a high preponderance of large families among Pakistanis and Bangladeshis, as illustrated in Figure 4.5.

It is also worth noting that households with three or more children formed 33 per cent of all Pakistani and Bangladeshi households in 2000/01, whereas they made up only 5 per cent of all households (see Figure 4.6). It is clear, then, that the issue of family size and its relationship with poverty remains a critical issue for these groups.

Low female economic activity rates

As well as the number of children a household may have to support, the number of incomes available to support them will be influenced by female economic activity rates. As families in Britain have increasingly moved towards a two-earner model, even if one of the earners may be part time, those families which assume a more traditional employment structure tend to have lower incomes. On the other hand, poverty may increase the domestic demands that are made on families rendering it less practicable for a partner to work. The absence of a washing machine, for example, particularly in a large household with a number of small children will create substantial work.[17] In the context of caring for a family and undertaking onerous domestic duties, undertaking paid work in addition may simply seem implausible.[18] Table 4.2 shows female economic activity rates by ethnic group in 2000/01, and illustrates the extremely low economic activity among Pakistani and Bangladeshi women, of whom nearly half are not in or seeking work due to looking after family and home. The economic inactivity rates of the other minority groups reveal that while their demographic profile means they have fewer women who are retired compared with the national average, they are all more likely to be looking after family or home, even if not to the extent of Bangladeshi and Pakistani women. The loss of potential adult earners in a family is likely to impact on their ability to meet what are considered normal standards of living in Britain.

An obvious question is the extent to which these traditional patterns of family life are changing, or whether a continuation of low female economic activity among Bangladeshi and Pakistani women, in particular, can be anticipated. The evidence suggests that over the last 15 years, excluding those women of retirement age, economic activity rates among Pakistani and Bangladeshi women of working age have increased from under a fifth of women to over a quarter.[19] Increases have been especially noted in the 25-30 age range in the decade from 1984 to 1993, and while activity rates drop dramatically on marriage, more highly educated Pakistani and Bangladeshi women are deferring marriage and thus continuing to work for longer.[20] So, while these rates remain well below those of other ethnic groups, there is some indication that we should not necessarily expect this pattern to be so pronounced in the future.

Table 4.2

Female economic activity and inactivity by ethnic group, 2000/01

	All women	Black groups	Indian	Pakistani and Bangladeshi	Other	White
	%	%	%	%	%	%
Economically active	**54**	**63**	**60**	**27**	**53**	**55**
of which:						
In full-time employment	31	41	44	14	35	31
In part-time employment	21	13	13	6	14	22
Unemployed	2	9	3	7	4	2
Economically inactive	**47**	**37**	**41**	**73**	**47**	**46**
of which:						
Retired	24	7	7	4	9	25
Student	2	6	2	3	9	1
Looking after family/home	10	13	18	47	17	9
Permanently sick or disabled	6	7	10	12	6	6
Temporarily sick or disabled	1	1	–	1	–	1
Other inactive	4	2	4	6	6	4

Source: Adapted from Department for Work and Pensions, *Family Resources Survey 2000/01*, 2002, Table 7.2

There continues, as well, to be debate about the extent to which low economic activity rates among Bangladeshi and Pakistani women reflect the
reality of their lives, with some claiming that the rates disguise work done
in the home or forms of sweated, and therefore unacknowledged, labour.
Others argue that there are no grounds for thinking that the economic
activity figures are a misrepresentation of these women's lives. Figures on
homeworking at the beginning of the 1980s, insofar as they could measure ethnicity, indicated that there was, if anything, an under-representation
of those from minority ethnic groups in this area.[21] On the other side, it is
worth noting Ballard's caution in relation to the Census returns of economic activity among Pakistani women. He describes the Census as
'notoriously poor at identifying activities in the domestic sector' and failing
to register the extensive amounts of homeworking among these women.[22]
Furthermore, a study carried out following the 1991 Census, which set out
to gain a substantial number of ethnic minority respondents within its sample, ended up with over half of its 338 respondents coming from minority
ethnic groups.[23] While this cannot inform us about national rates of homeworking it does suggest on the one hand that ethnic minority homeworking is not necessarily 'hidden', though it may remain not very easily
susceptible to analysis through standard surveys or the Census. On the
other hand, it indicates that the suggestions from local, qualitative studies
of greater prevalence among minority ethnic groups have some basis.
Such studies have drawn attention, in particular, to practices of homeworking among Pakistani women, particularly those with existing family
responsibilities. Afshar drew attention to homeworking in her study of
Pakistani women in West Yorkshire,[24] and Brah's Birmingham respondents both provided evidence of some homeworking and discussed the
idea of the perceived dishonour connected with working outside the
home, without, though, indicating that it was an overwhelming constraint.[25] Young Muslim women would appear, it seems, to be rejecting
homeworking as an appropriate employment option.[26]

It remains, however, very hard to obtain categorical evidence on the
prevalence of homeworking and how it varies with ethnic group and
whether hidden or unobserved homeworking is a factor in the reported
low economic activity rates among women. Alternative ways of understanding Pakistani and Bangladeshi women's low economic activity rates
draw attention to the relevance of poor qualifications and/or limited knowledge of English in limiting their economic activity.[27] Dale and others, while
acknowledging the importance of fluency in English in patterns of economic activity, have also described the ways in which the domestic role is

not only sufficiently arduous on its own, but can also be perceived as a positive choice.[28] A further factor that may repay consideration is the high self-employment rates among, in particular, Pakistani men. Those in self-employment often require, or benefit from, additional support at home, which may create an extra demand on wives, while not necessarily being perceived as economic activity. The issue of economic activity in relation to labour market possibilities is discussed further in Chapter 5.

Female economic activity rates are often cited as a cultural aspect of particular groups' experience, with low rates reflecting a preference for retaining women in the home and in a more traditional role among certain minorities. Other forms of explanation might relate female economic activity rates more closely to the overall labour market experience of particular groups and the factors associated with limited labour market opportunities more broadly. These include qualification levels, access to particular types of work, including part-time and service sector work, the 'costs' associated with finding work in high unemployment or multi-disadvantaged areas, and, importantly, the trade-off between benefit receipt and employment in low-pay occupations and where one partner is already out of work.[29] Chapters 5 and 6 consider the explanations for minority groups' poverty rates in terms of their relationship with the labour market and the benefits system.

Notes

1   T Warnes, 'The Age Structure and Ageing of the Ethnic Groups' in D Coleman and J Salt (eds), *Ethnicity in the 1991 Census: Volume One: demographic characteristics of the ethnic minority populations*, HMSO, 1996

2   D Owen, 'Size, Structure and Growth of the Ethnic Minority Populations' in D Coleman and J Salt (eds), *Ethnicity in the 1991 Census: Volume One: demographic characteristics of the ethnic minority populations*, HMSO, 1996

3   A Scott, D Pearce and P Goldslatt, 'The Sizes and Characteristics of the Minority Ethnic Populations of Great Britain – latest estimates', *Population Trends* 105, National Statistics, Autumn 2001, pp6–15

4   For the purposes of the table I have not only combined black other with black Caribbean, but I have also for the *Labour Force Survey* estimates added in the black mixed group, following recommended practice. I have also combined the *Labour Force Survey* categories of other-other (non-mixed) and other-mixed. However, this means that some of those who would formerly have been in other Asian will no longer be in other Asian (non-mixed) so I have had to keep those two categories separate. The introduction of mixed categories may also have had some impact on the Indian, Pakistani and Bangladeshi categories.

5   R Berthoud, 'Family Formation in Multi-Cultural Britain: three patterns of diversity', Paper 2000-34, *Working Papers of the Institute for Social and Economic Research*, University of Essex, 2000, p12

6   In this light it may be relevant to note that inter-ethnic unions are more common for men from minority ethnic groups than for minority group women. There are differences between groups, however, with inter-ethnic unions overall less common among those from South Asian groups (A Berrington, 'Marriage Patterns and Inter-Ethnic Unions' in D Coleman and J Salt (eds), *Ethnicity in the 1991 Census: Volume one: demographic characteristics of the ethnic minority populations*, HMSO, 1996, p180)

7   M Boneham, 'Shortchanging' Black and Minority Ethnic Elders', in J Bradshaw and R Sainsbury (eds), *Experiencing Poverty*, Ashgate, 2000

8   See Chapter 6 and L Platt, 'Social Security in a Multi-Ethnic Society' in J Millar (ed), *Understanding Social Security: issues for social policy and practice*, The Policy Press, forthcoming 2003, for a discussion of the relationship between minority ethnic groups and social security.

9   See note 7, p170

10 See note 1, pp173-174, for a summary of extant research on this subject.

11 See note 7, p175

12 L Platt and M Noble, *Race, Place and Poverty*, Joseph Rowntree Foundation, 1999

13 See note 5

14 See note 5

15 See note 5, p19

16 L Platt, 'Ethnicity and Inequality: British children's experience of means-tested benefits', *Journal of Comparative Family Studies*, forthcoming 2003

17 A Brah, ''Race' and 'Culture' in the Gendering of Labour Markets: South Asian young Muslim women and the labour market', *New Community* 19.3, 1993. In this article, Brah also illustrates the extent to which 'work' encompasses both paid and unpaid work in the perception of her respondents, in contrast to the conventional discourse, which also dominates at the policy level.

18 A Brah and S Shaw, *Working Choices: South Asian young women and the labour market*, Department of Employment Research Report 91, 1992

19 F Sly, T Thair and A Risdon, 'Labour Market Participation of Ethnic Groups', *Labour Market Trends*, December 1998, Table 8

20 K Bhopal, 'How Gender and Ethnicity Intersect: the significance of education, employment and marital status', *Sociological Research Online*, 3.3, 1998, available at http://www.socresonline.org.uk/socresonline/3/3/6.html

21 C Hakim, *Home-based Work in Great Britain: a report of the 1981 National Homeworking Survey and the DE research programme on homework,*

Department of Employment Research Paper, 1987

22 R Ballard, 'The Pakistanis: stability and introspection' in C Peach (ed), *Ethnicity in the 1991 Census: Volume Two: the ethnic minority populations of Great Britain*, HMSO, 1996, p135

23 A Felstead and N Jewson with J Goodwin, *Homeworkers in Britain*, DTI and DfEE, 1996

24 H Afshar, 'Gender Roles and the 'Moral Economy of Kin' among Pakistani Women in West Yorkshire', *New Community* 15.2, 1989; see also, A Phizaklea and C Wolkowitz, *Homeworking Women: gender, racism and class at work*, Sage, 1993

25 See note 17

26 See note 18

27 T Modood 'Education' in T Modood, R Berthoud *et al*, *Ethnic Minorities in Britain: diversity and disadvantage*, Policy Studies Institute, 1997; see also note 18

28 A Dale, E Fieldhouse, N Shaheen and V Kalra, 'The Labour Market Prospects for Pakistani and Bangladeshi Women', *Work, Employment and Society* 16.1, 2002

29 T Modood 'Employment' in T Modood, R Berthoud *et al*, *Ethnic Minorities in Britain: diversity and disadvantage*; see also P Gregg and J Wadsworth, 'More Work in Fewer Households?' in J Hills, *New Inequalities: the changing distribution of income and wealth in the United Kingdom*, CUP, 1996

Five

Explaining ethnic minority poverty: structural and labour market-related explanations

As the current government is at pains to point out, much of the solution to poverty can be found in the labour market. A reasonably well-paid and secure job not only enables current needs to be met, but can support a family, enable it to weather crises, and provide the means to save for old age. Unemployment, particularly persistent unemployment, insecurity, and low pay, by contrast, can lead not just to present want but to multiple deprivation, and to a poor old age.

This chapter outlines the labour market position of Britain's minority ethnic groups. It reveals the different levels of disadvantage that they face in the areas of employment sector, pay and unemployment and it explores some of the factors that are known to contribute to poorer position in the labour market, such as concentration in areas of high unemployment, youth, and lack of sufficient human capital – or educational qualifications. It outlines how much we can explain by these means and how much of the disadvantage experienced by ethnic minority groups is left unexplained, before reflecting on the role of discrimination in employment.

To start this consideration of structural (as opposed to cultural) factors as they affect minority ethnic groups, this chapter first outlines the particular immigration experience of the different minority groups. It describes how this experience has resulted in particular areas of geographical and occupational concentration and segregation, and the consequent differential impact of the processes of deindustrialisation, which took place through the 1970s and the 1980s.

Immigration patterns

Those of Indian ethnicity were, according to the 1991 Census, the largest specified minority group (though if it had been possible to enumerate those of Irish ethnicity they would probably have exceeded the Indian group). Indians made up 1.5 per cent of the population, and this had grown to around 1.7 per cent of the population by 2000, as Table 4.1 showed. They thus exceed the proportion made up by Caribbeans. While there have been Indians in Britain for centuries, the numbers remained small until the post-war period, when Indian immigration increased, enabled by cheaper travel and encouraged by labour shortages and existing settlers who could supply information and ease transition in Britain.[1] Immigrants were largely young men, and, as has often been emphasised, came to Britain with the intention of returning once the intended achievements had been fulfilled. The restrictions of the 1962 Commonwealth Immigrants Act transmuted the pattern of immigration, with family reunification taking over from primary immigration and the plan of return being substantially abandoned.

The removal of rights of residence from Kenyan Asians in 1967 and Amin's expulsion in 1972 of the Ugandan Asians (the majority of whom define themselves as ethnically Indian) introduced a further phase of political immigration. Thus the bulk of Indian immigration took place between the mid-1950s and the mid-1970s, later than Caribbean, but earlier than the bulk of Pakistani immigration. The resulting age profile is biased towards the younger adult ages, but not so much towards children's ages, as in the Pakistani and Bangladeshi profiles. The smaller ratio of numbers of children to adults and the fact that political refugees arrived with their families also means that fewer Indians than Pakistanis are British-born (42 per cent compared with 50 per cent). Unlike the Vietnamese refugees, who also arrived following expulsion from their homes on account of their ethnicity, the expelled Ugandan families were predominantly skilled and educated, with experience in business and a good command of English. Though they were not necessarily able to exploit these assets (nor many of their financial assets in Uganda) following their departure, these attributes would appear to have affected the outcomes for subsequent generations.

At the broad level, Indians are concentrated within the South East, especially outer London, the West Midlands and the East Midlands. Even within those broad areas, however, they tend to be dispersed, though there is some evidence that choices expressed through owner occupation are leading to the development of relatively affluent Indian communities with higher than expected concentrations.[2] As this book shows, the Indian ethnic group is now performing as well as, or better than, the white group in a number of income-related areas.

In the pre-partition era, there was a small but continuous Indian population in Britain. However, mass migration from the sub-continent coincided with the post-partition era. Thus, Pakistani migration, from both East and West Pakistan, but especially West Pakistan and Mirpur in particular, started in the late 1950s and peaked in 1961 – partly in anticipation of the 1962 Commonwealth Immigrants Act. Over the next ten years the number of Pakistanis arriving as workers declined while this type of migrant was substantially overtaken by arrivals of dependants of those already resident. Dependants continued to arrive throughout the 1970s but at a slower rate. As well as those from Mirpur and other parts of the Punjab, these migrants also included a number of Pathans and Muhajirs. All of these groups continue to retain distinct identities within Britain. In addition, prior to the civil war of 1971 they also included Bengalis from East Bengal who subsequently became Bangladeshi with the establishment of the separate state. As with Indians, therefore, the category of Pakistani includes numerous cultural and ethnic groups. The increasing stringency of immigration controls served to delay, but not prevent, family reunification, so that it took place later than for Indian families at slow rates over time. The vast majority of those Pakistanis aged under 20 in 1991 were born in Britain. This will be even more the case by 2001. In contrast, the vast majority of those aged 30 and over in 1991 were not born in Britain. The age distribution of Pakistanis is overwhelmingly weighted in favour of children, reflecting the high fertility of Pakistani families.

Pakistanis in Britain are quite highly concentrated, predominantly in the West Midlands, Lancashire, West Yorkshire and Greater Manchester. The largest Pakistani population is in Birmingham, where, in 1991, they made up 6.9 per cent of the population, but there are also significant concentrations in Lancashire and Yorkshire. Attracted to work in the textile industry of Northern towns, they also went to work in the metalworking and car manufacturing industries in Birmingham. In this latter town the industries remained healthy throughout the 1970s, when immigration was still taking place, and their pattern of residence reflects aspects of the timing of their immigration.

In 1971 East Pakistan, which had come into being as part of Pakistan in 1947, seceded and became the independent state of

Bangladesh. Up to that point, those immigrating from what became Bangladesh were included among Pakistanis in British estimates and counts of post-war immigration.[4] It is clear that Bangladeshi immigration is more recent than the bulk of Pakistani and Indian immigration. While primary immigration had taken place during the 1960s and 1970s, total immigration peaked in the 1980s due to family reunification. The minority ethnic group expanded quickly as children were born in this country to the growing population. Nevertheless, Bangladeshis formed the smallest minority group in 1991, but the population has continued to expand since 1991, overtaking the Chinese group by 2000. Given its high fertility and young profile, the group will continue to grow, as was identified in the discussion in the previous chapter. The Bangladeshi population in Britain is the most geographically concentrated of the minority groups. In 1991 nearly a quarter of the total British Bangladeshi population lived in Tower Hamlets,[5] and an estimated four-fifths lived in London as a whole in 2000.[6]

Caribbean is my chosen name for the composite group of those who respond or are allocated to either black Caribbean or black other categories, (as discussed in Chapter 2). While there was a small Caribbean presence in Britain in the first half of the twentieth century, the bulk of the growth in this population took place during the 1950s and 1960s with the attempt to fill the labour shortage with Commonwealth workers. This phase of immigration has been marked as beginning with the docking of the *Windrush* in 1948.[7] After 1971, this population does not appear to have expanded significantly, immigration having come to a standstill by 1975 and births being compensated for by outward and return migration.[8] However, the combination of the black Caribbean and black other categories results in some implied growth in the last decade. Taking the black other group into account, the vast majority of Caribbeans are British-born and have a youthful demographic profile relative to the population as a whole, though not to other minority groups. The Caribbeans made up, in 1991, 1.2 per cent of the population of Britain. If combined with 'black mixed' for the most recent estimates, this population increased to roughly 1.5 per cent of the population by 2000 (Table 4.1). They settled in manufacturing centres in the North West, Yorkshire and the West Midlands, which still see some concentrations, but the biggest settlement took place in London and over half the group was resident in London in 2000.

Black African is one of the more heterogeneous of the groups classified. Those who defined themselves as black African in the 1991 Census were found to come from 53 different countries (including Caribbean countries), and over a third were British born.[9] There have been African residents in Britain for centuries, with communities built around seamen in major ports. However, immigration from African countries increased in the late 1940s to 1960s, largely for education and later, in the 1980s and 1990s, more for asylum. The black African population made up 0.4 per cent of the population in 1991 and was largely concentrated in Liverpool, Cardiff, Leeds and, especially, London.[10] In 2000 nearly 80 per cent of black Africans were living in London. By 2000, the black African population was estimated to have approximately doubled, making up 0.8 per cent of the population (see Table 4.1). The population is a very youthful one with nearly 30 per cent below the age of 16. It is also a group with one of the highest levels of qualifications. Yet for this group, even more than others, those qualifications do not translate into economic welfare.

According to the 1991 Census, the Chinese population was, with the Bangladeshi group, the smallest specified minority group, at under 0.3 per cent of the population. If the Vietnamese, with their distinct immigration history, are separated out from the group,[11] it is becomes yet smaller. Despite established settlements in Liverpool, London and Cardiff from the nineteenth century, the total number of Chinese in Britain did not exceed 5,000 people up to the period of post-war migration. Under the Nationality Act of 1948, Hong Kong Chinese had rights of settlement in the UK. Those who came in this period were able to sponsor others to follow, thus setting up the pattern of chain migration characteristic of this group. That this process of chain migration continued slowly but steadily is indicated by the proportion of the Chinese born in Britain, which, at 28 per cent, is lower than that of any other specified group. The arrival of students from mainland China in the 1980s has also had an effect on the proportion born in Britain and the age structure of the Chinese. Apart from a certain concentration in London, the Chinese population is widely dispersed throughout the country. The majority of the Vietnamese in Britain are those of Chinese ethnicity who came as political refugees from persecution from 1975 onwards. These refugees were received as part of an international settlement effort to disperse them from Hong Kong. Those who came to the UK had rarely positively selected it as their destination and, despite the active settlement procedure, acquiring fluency in English was an obstacle to employment, as was the shortage of skills that the refugees held that were readily usable in the British labour market.[12] Reception centres set up to accommodate the refugees on arrival were designed to disperse the refugees, but there has been some movement to major centres of population since, resulting in relatively large Vietnamese communities in London and Birmingham. The Census country of birth information shows that half of those born in Vietnam defined themselves as Chinese in 1991 and half ended up in the other Asian category. Despite a substantial proportion of the Chinese category being made up of the Vietnamese Chinese, given its history and background this latter group is likely to differ from other Chinese in terms of outcomes and life-chances. However, anecdotal evidence of a strong commitment to education and formal educational achievement indicates that that could change over time. Already the outcomes of the Chinese group indicate that, along with the Indians it is developing an increasingly successful profile at both occupational and educational levels.

Employment sector, pay and unemployment

The differences in minority groups' immigration history – its timing, the sector in which the group became established, the geographical area in which they became established and the reasons for immigration affecting the skills and experience they brought with them – have contributed to different employment and unemployment experiences for the groups.

The forced migration of the East African Asians and the Vietnamese Chinese has resulted in two different patterns. For the East African Asians there have been comparatively successful outcomes, particularly in the second generation where they have been able to make more of their parents' entrepreneurial and business skills and commitment to education. By contrast, the Vietnamese did not bring with them familiarity with English or skills that are so easily marketable in the British labour market and have been less successful in finding opportunities in Britain.

Pakistani immigration was focused towards labour intensive, low-skill industries, which has left the group concentrated in high unemployment areas of former industrial centres following de-industrialisation. They have been tied to such locations by the poor quality owner occupied housing in undesirable locations in which they had little option but to settle in the years of immigration, where high housing competition was an aspect of areas of high employment that were seeking labour. Nevertheless, they have perhaps adapted more successfully to de-industrialisation and the transition to a service economy than might have been anticipated on the basis of previous heavy concentration in manufacturing.[13]

The Chinese, on immigration, developed their employment niche predominantly in catering, finding successful chain migration worked with lower concentrations and a more dispersed profile. By contrast Bangladeshi immigration, peaking as it did following the decline of manufacturing, resulted in both an intense geographical concentration and yet also followed a sectoral concentration in catering and distribution. The concentrations in particular sectors have come about partly through the opportunities that were offered at times of immigration and partly through the way immigration depended, following the 1962 Act, on sponsorship in particular industries.

In subsequent periods, some of the sectoral concentration established through original migration patterns has been retained: Chinese and Bangladeshis continued to show massive concentrations in the catering industry. In 1991 55 per cent of the Chinese worked in distribution and catering, chiefly in restaurants and cafés, with a large number of the remainder working in other services and banking. They were under-represented in semi-skilled or unskilled manual jobs.[14] Two-thirds of Bangladeshis worked in distribution and catering, the majority of 'Indian' restaurants being Bangladeshi-run. They were consequently under-represented in other industries and overwhelmingly concentrated in manual occupations.[15]

Pakistanis had worked predominantly in the heavy manufacturing and textile industries of Birmingham and Yorkshire up to the early 1980s, but the recession of that period hit these industries particularly hard and alternatives were not readily available. By 1991 roughly a third of employed men were working in distribution and catering and there had also been a shift into transport (such as taxi driving and chauffeuring), while they remained slightly over-represented in manufacturing compared to the white population.[16]

Having come to Britain initially to take up jobs in the service industries, especially hospitals and transport as well as in the ailing manufacturing sectors, and with many women having been recruited directly as nurses, Caribbeans showed differences in 1991 in their social class position according to sex. Black Caribbean men in 1991 were over-represented in manual occupations, with many in the construction industry, whereas female occupations were comparable to their white counterparts (even though they experienced higher rates of unemployment).[17]

Indians in 1991 shared with the Chinese high rates of self-employment. Their over-representation in the managerial and professional social classes was, however, also balanced by an over-representation in semi-skilled manual occupations.[18]

More recent work from the *Labour Force Survey* suggests that these patterns and concentrations have largely persisted.[19] In 1998-2000, 44 per cent of Chinese men were employed in the restaurant industry and 52 per cent of Bangladeshi employees and self employed worked in this sector. One in eight Pakistani men were by this time driving cabs or working as chauffeurs. An Indian man's probability of being in the medical profession was ten times the national average; and they had the highest representation of all groups in the top two social classes with 47 per cent concentrated here. Chinese men were also over-represented in the higher social classes (44 per cent compared to around 40 percent among white and black African groups), while Pakistanis and Bangladeshis were under-represented at the top of the class scale. Indian and Pakistani women were more likely than other women to be employed in manufacturing, especially textiles, as well as in retail. Caribbean and African women were, instead, concentrated in health and social care work.

Pay

Occupational and sectoral differences will affect the levels of pay that the different minority ethnic groups achieve. This may explain some of the disparity in pay, which found Pakistani and Bangladeshi men and women earning the least of all groups averaging at £6.87 an hour for men and £6.33 an hour for women in 1998. This compared with £9.00 an hour nationally among Indian, white and Chinese men.[20] How far can these rates be related to the occupations of the different groups? Hotel and restaurant work had the most extensive rates of low pay in 1998.[21] However, the largest numbers of low-paid workers were found in wholesale and retail work, as well as substantial proportions of the low paid coming from health and social work, and manufacturing, as well as hotels and restaurants. The Low Pay Commission identified ethnic minority groups as at increased risk of low pay and found that, even within low-paid sectors such as hotels and restaurants, Pakistani and Bangladeshi workers were more likely than their counterparts to be under-paid.[22] Homeworking was also identified as a source of low pay, and as an area that was likely to affect women from South Asian minority groups, in particular. Felstead and Jewson found that even within the low-paid homeworking sector, the hourly pay for women was lower than for men and for women from minority ethnic groups was lower than for white women. The lowest hourly rate was received by black Caribbean women.[23]

The pay of those working in the manual sector is much lower than for those working in the non-manual sector. According to *The New Earnings Survey*, in 2000 full-time manual earnings averaged £7.43 an hour, with full-time non-manual earnings £11.81 an hour. For men the gap was particularly pronounced with an average difference between full-time manual and non-manual earnings of nearly £6 an hour. And this excludes those who earn less than the national insurance limit and, therefore, underestimates the extent of low wages. Occupation will thus affect the amount of income available to the household, even before other factors come into play.

However, Blackaby and others investigated earning and employment differentials between groups taking into account the fact that a high proportion of ethnic minorities live in London which has untypically high wage rates.[24] They therefore controlled for region as well as for whether the minority was born in the UK and for age structure. Doing this they found substantial wage differentials with a gap of over £1.80 per hour between white and black groups in the period 1993-96. They concluded that 'ethnic differences in labour market remuneration cannot be explained as a characteristic problem – such as poor qualifications, and an unfavourable regional and industrial distribution'.

Unemployment

The employment sectors in which groups are concentrated will affect not only their income, but also their employment chances, their residence and their mobility. Unemployment rates are higher than overall in manufacturing and construction and, for men, in distribution, hotels and restaurants. The *Labour Force Survey* showed that unemployment rates for those in manual occupations were more than double the rates for those from non-manual occupations; and this was broadly true for both men and women.[25] The large job losses that have afflicted the textile industries in recent years have impacted more heavily on women and in particular Indian and Pakistani women.

To this extent, the probability of poverty consequent on unemployment can partly be explained by the occupational patterns of some minority groups. It cannot, however, fully explain the huge disparities in unemployment between groups. The *Labour Force Survey* reveals the huge differences in unemployment rates experienced by those from different ethnic groups. Worklessness is a critical cause of poverty and the figures shown in Table 5.1 go some way to making the link between ethnicity and excess poverty. The numbers in the table are also illustrated graphically in Figures 5.1 and 5.2, which help to draw out some of the contrasts in unemployment and economic activity. Table 5.1 illustrates the excess unemployment experienced by all minority groups and by both the men and women in those minority groups. Even Indians, who have high educational levels and who are relatively successful in many occupational aspects, continued to experience higher rates of unemployment than the population as a whole. Caribbean, black African and Pakistani unemployment rates were three times the proportion in the population, while the unemployment of Bangladeshis was in a different league, with a quarter of the economically active Bangladeshi population suffering unemployment.

There are also some differences by gender. While women's unemployment overall pursued rates below those of male unemployment, for

Table 5.1

Patterns of economic activity and unemployment in the UK, Autumn 1999/00

	Economic activity rate			ILO unemployment rate		
	All	Men	Women	All	Men	Women
Caribbean	68	70	66	15	18	12**
Black African	66	73	60	15	14	17
Indian	65	75	54	7	7	8
Pakistani	50	71	28	16	15	20
Bangladeshi	43	61	22	25	20	24***
Chinese	57	62	54	*	*	*
Other	63	73	53	12	13	11
White	64	72	56	5	6	5
All groups	64	72	55	6	6	5

Notes

* = sample size too small for reliable estimates

** = based just on black Caribbean estimate as black other sample size was too small for reliable estimates

*** = based on the aggregate Pakistani and Bangladeshi female unemployment rate as the Bangladeshi unemployment sample size was too small for reliable estimates

ILO unemployment rate refers to the proportion of the economically active population who were unemployed and either seeking work or waiting to take up a job.

Source: Adapted from B Twomey, 'Labour Market Participation of Ethnic Groups', *Labour Market Trends*, January 2001, Table 3

most minority groups unemployment rates were higher among women. The major exception to this was among Caribbean women, whose unemployment rates, while over twice those of white women, were nevertheless six percentage points lower than rates for Caribbean men. This is a further aspect of Caribbean women's distinct profile in labour market terms, along with high economic activity rates (despite the high rates of lone parenthood, discussed in Chapter 4). Their educational profile is also distinct, with higher levels of qualifications among Caribbean women than among Caribbean men, a feature which again distinguishes them from women from other minority groups.

The economic activity rates for Pakistani and Bangladeshi women illustrate their contrasting patterns of behaviour compared with the other groups. But this means that the high unemployment rates for Pakistanis and Bangladeshis are particularly striking given that they have the lowest economic activity rates among working-age adults of any group. Their

Figure 5.1

Economic activity by ethnicity and gender, 1999/00

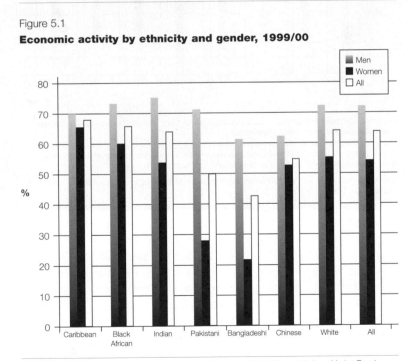

Source: Derived from B Twomey, 'Labour Market Participation of Ethnic Groups', *Labour Market Trends*, January 2001, Table 3

Figure 5.2

Unemployment by ethnicity and gender, 1999/00

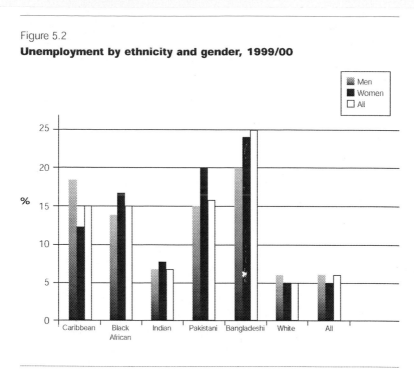

Notes

The female Caribbean unemployment rate is based just on the black Caribbean estimate as black other sample size was too small for reliable estimates.

The female Bangladeshi unemployment rate is based on the aggregate Pakistani and Bangladeshi female unemployment rate as the Bangladeshi unemployment sample size was too small for reliable estimates. It is therefore an understatement of the 'true' Bangladeshi unemployment rate.

Source: Derived from B Twomey, 'Labour Market Participation of Ethnic Groups', *Labour Market Trends*, January 2001, Table 3

employment rate is thus only 46 and 35 per cent respectively among working-age adults, compared with 75 per cent among all working-age adults. This is again differentiated by sex, so that male Pakistani and Bangladeshi employment is 65 and 52 per cent respectively, compared with 80 per cent in the population as a whole. Female employment rates are even more dramatically lower than in the population as a whole: while 70 per cent of all working-age women are employed, only 25 per cent of Pakistani women and 15 per cent of Bangladeshi women are in employ-ment. While part of the low economic activity can be explained by low female economic activity, as discussed above, men from these groups also have low economic activity rates relative to men from other groups, which suggests that explanations of economic activity rates based simply on traditional cultural patterns are insufficient.

So having identified these huge differences in worklessness between ethnic groups, how can we hope to explain them? We can resort, in part, to demography: lower economic activity rates can be a consequence of the more youthful profile of this group with, therefore, higher proportions in full-time education. It is also a reflection of the longer duration of education among minority groups compared to the population as a whole, an issue covered further below.[26] Thus, while Pakistani and Bangladeshi 16–24-year-olds are less likely than other minority groups to be in full-time education, they are nevertheless 10 per cent more likely to be so than the average for all 16–24-year-olds. Thus the high rates in education combined with the high proportions of Pakistanis and Bangladeshis in this age range will have an impact on the groups' overall economic activity rates. On the other hand, among Pakistani women, economic activity rates are *highest* among 16–19-year-olds, indicating both a lower tendency to pursue education and also the impact of marriage in reducing economic activity.[27] This pattern may change over time as women stay on in education and consequently defer marriage until later.[28]

It was shown in Chapter 3 how low income and deprivation show substantial variation by area, and how minority ethnic groups displayed distinct patterns of geographical settlement. Unemployment rates also vary substantially by area, and so part of the explanation for the current large differences in unemployment can be sought in the over-representation of minority ethnic groups in high unemployment areas. Unemployment is typically higher in inner urban areas where minority groups are likely to be concentrated. In particular, inner London has both high unemployment rates relative to the rest of the country and very high concentrations of certain minority groups. For example, a vast majority of black Africans live in inner London, which could contribute to their excess unemployment, which is three times the overall unemployment rate. But the geographical effect can only form a partial explanation since their unemployment rate in inner London in 1998/99 was still twice that of the white group.[29]

A further factor which may affect differential unemployment rates between groups may be found in the fact that unemployment itself is associated more with younger ages, particularly for men. For example, it could be argued that the high rates of male Caribbean unemployment can in part be explained by high unemployment rates among young men and the large number of young Caribbean men available for work. This contention has been investigated and it has been found that the unemployment rates of young Caribbean men in the mid 1990s were not only four times the overall unemployment rate, but were even twice the rate of other young men, at 20 per cent compared with roughly 10 per cent.[30] Figures for 1999/00 confirm this picture, with rates of 29 per cent unemployment for black Caribbean men aged 16 to 24 compared with 14 per cent for all men in this age group.[31] This compares with unemployment rates of 21 per cent among Pakistanis in this age group and of 17 per cent for young Indians. The experience of *young* black men is, therefore, extreme, and begs explanation. On the other hand, among young women, the highest rates are found among Pakistani 16–24-year-olds with unemployment rates reaching a massive 38 per cent of the group in 1999/00.[32] Pakistani women's increased levels of economic activity at this age, then, result in extraordinarily high rates of unemployment. The intersection of gender effects with ethnicity and, presumably, with limited levels of qualifications for those who leave school at 16, results in poor employment prospects. In this situation, marriage and withdrawal from a hostile labour market may seem a more viable option, independent of family or cultural constraints.[33]

A further impact on unemployment may also be the consequence of apparent lack of opportunities and the experience of labour market discrimination (an issue discussed below). It has been suggested that negative experiences and expectations may result in detachment from the labour market; but recent research by Thomas has contradicted such 'cultural' explanations.[34] Thomas tested whether attitudes could be seen to have an impact on employment duration, and specifically the differences in employment duration among those from different ethnic groups. The analysis demonstrated that, rather, when taking account of attitudes, the gap between the probabilities of exit from unemployment between white groups and Indians and Pakistanis and Bangladeshis actually increased.[35] That is, these groups held a greater attachment to the labour market and commitment to finding work than their chances of escaping unemployment warranted. Disengagement from the labour market cannot then be used to explain worse unemployment experience among those from particular minority groups.

The differential unemployment associated with youth may explain some of the differences in labour market outcomes and therefore poverty; and the low economic activity of women may give us some way of understanding the differences, but neither of these can fully explain the disparities. Moreover, high youth unemployment rates may themselves have impacts throughout the life course, contributing to long-term poverty or social exclusion. Can it, however, be assumed that minority groups are bringing the same educational experience to bear in their engagement with the labour market, or is their labour market experience a consequence of differential educational attainment and attachment?

Education

Experience of unemployment and employment opportunities will them-selves be influenced by the skills and experience of the individual, their area of residence, their possibilities for mobility, their command of English and, of course, discrimination both direct and indirect, in selection processes and in the workplace. For the younger generations the qualifications that they have acquired *should* be critical in determining their relative success, but the extent to which they affect groups equally is in question. There follows a consideration of the role of education in mitigating or exacerbating disadvantage.

The fundamental question in relation to poverty and members of minority groups' experiences across the life course is the extent to which educational outcomes translate into labour market disadvantage. A potential source of concern is poor educational outcomes translating into poor labour market outcomes. This would imply that policies should be focused on mitigating educational disadvantage and equalising the impact of schooling. It also leads to a consideration of the extent to which New Deal and labour market insertion programmes are successful and to what extent they result in different outcomes for different groups. On the other hand, evidence that educational qualifications fail to translate into positive labour market outcomes for some groups will imply that attention should be focused on combating discrimination or the 'ethnic penalty' – an issue discussed in the final part of this chapter. Cross-cutting this discussion will be the relevance of social class background and the continuing evidence that class background remains a critical factor in labour market and life course outcomes.

At the same time, while the current position of some minority ethnic groups may not indicate that education is necessarily the most powerful route to overcome poverty and disadvantage, it not only plays a part but it is also likely to be more significant for future generations in the context of increasing qualifications levels in the population as a whole. Education may not be *sufficient* to counteract the disadvantage, but it is likely to be *necessary* if that is to be a possibility.

Educational achievement

When comparing educational achievements there are a number of issues to consider. Firstly, at what age educational achievement is being compared: if it is being compared across groups as a whole at a time when levels of educational achievement among school leavers are rising, to what extent will the age profile of the group determine the qualifications? That is, you would expect older groups to have lower levels of qualifications. A related issue for minority groups is the question of where people acquired their qualifications, and whether qualifications acquired in their country of origin have the same currency in the UK at the time of immigration, or whether we should separate out the migrant generation from those born in Britain. Modood investigated this alongside the question of to what extent successive generations are improving on the educational level of their parents' generation.[36] An alternative is to compare educational levels among particular age cohorts, such as 18–year-olds. In this case, however, any delays in acquiring qualifications may mean that the comparison is slightly skewed. Such a comparison does, though, enable some evaluation of how different groups are faring within the school system. This, of course, is complicated by the continuing evidence of the impact of social class background on educational levels, in part related to the area issues discussed above. It is, therefore, also necessary to look at the interaction between social class and ethnicity when considering ethnic group differences in achievement.

Table 5.2 illustrates that more than a fifth of working-age adults now have a higher (ie, above 'A' level) qualification, while under a fifth have no qualifications. While there is some discrepancy between men and women, with women having slightly lower qualifications levels, this pattern is more pronounced for some minority groups. The table shows the particularly high qualifications levels for Africans and Chinese, with Chinese women being slightly better qualified than Chinese men, but a substantially higher proportion of black African men having higher qualifications compared to black African women. Indian men also tend to be highly qualified, but there is again a substantial gap between them and Indian women. Caribbean women are the only group where the women's qualification levels are markedly greater than those of the men. This will in part reflect the recruitment patterns of the original generation, where qualified women were recruited directly into health service occupations. The relatively poor achievement of Caribbean men nevertheless stands out. While this cannot be related specifically to timing of immigration and immigration

Table 5.2
Percentage of working-age people at different qualifications levels by ethnic group, average for 1996-98.

	Higher qualification	Other qualification	No qualification
All			
All groups	22	61	17
White	22	61	16
Caribbean	19	62	19
Black African	32	56	12
Indian	25	57	18
Pakistani	13	54	32
Bangladeshi	8	48	44
Chinese	29	52	19
Men			
All groups	23	62	15
White	22	62	14
Caribbean	15	62	23
Black African	40	51	9
Indian	29	57	15
Pakistani	17	56	27
Bangladeshi	10	51	39
Chinese	28	53	20
Women			
All groups	21	60	19
White	21	60	19
Caribbean	22	62	16
Black African	25	61	15
Indian	20	58	22
Pakistani	10	52	38
Bangladeshi	Insufficient sample size	45	49
Chinese	30	52	18

Source: Adapted from B Twomey, 'Labour Market Participation of Ethnic Groups', *Labour Market Trends*, January 2001, Table 2

history, it may be that it reflects the traditional concentration of Caribbeans in construction, and other relatively low-skilled manual sectors. The perpetuation of such 'under-achievement' among subsequent genera-tions, for whom such occupations are less available, may reflect more,

however, on within-school experiences of groups, as well as on the reproduction of social class patterns, as the discussion of the current cohort of
18–year-olds, below, considers. Overall, though, Caribbean qualifications
are very close to those of the total population, suggesting perhaps a certain degree of convergence. Looking at the least qualified groups, 32 per
cent of Pakistanis and 44 per cent of Bangladeshis (and nearly half of
Bangladeshi women) are without any qualifications. While these two
groups remain linked together as the least qualified groups, the differences between them are nevertheless substantial.[37] If length of stay in
Britain is the cause of the differences, then it suggests that Bangladeshi
qualifications levels should improve, as they already seem to be doing to
a certain extent. However, if the timing of migration is critical, and the levels of concentration within the deprived areas that are a feature of the settlement patterns of Bangladeshis, then the outlook for the Bangladeshis
may be less optimistic.

   The differences in educational level illustrated in Table 5.2 approximately map onto the patterns of poverty and differences between minority ethnic groups illustrated in Chapter 2, with Chinese and Indians
relatively advantaged and Pakistanis and Bangladeshis relatively disadvantaged. They show that, roughly speaking, those with the greatest disadvantage also have the lowest levels of qualifications, but they do not
indicate the direction of effects. Nor can they reveal what value education
has in securing positive socio-economic outcomes. Additionally, they do
not explain the disadvantaged position of black Africans, where both men
and women have above average levels of higher qualifications.

Trends in achievement

There have been huge changes in patterns of education since the 1960s.
At that time the majority of pupils left school at the age of 15 to take up
employment. Now 70 per cent of 16–year-olds and nearly three-fifths of
17-year-olds are in post-compulsory education.[38] Between 1961/62 and
1996/97 the proportion of those of school leaving age achieving the equivalent of five GCSEs grades A to C rose from 14 per cent to 45 per cent.
Both boys and girls have made, and continue to make, substantial gains
in levels of qualifications, although girls' performance has for some years
now outstripped that of boys. In 1998/99 55 per cent of girls and 44 per
cent of boys gained five or more GCSEs at grades A to C; similar increasing success can be seen at 'A' level, with over 37 per cent of the relevant

age band of girls and 30 per cent of boys achieving two or more 'A' levels.

Given that qualifications are increasing in the population, it can be anticipated that within-group differences may reduce over time. One way of exploring this point is to consider the experience of the 'migrant' and 'born in Britain' generations, and what effect the experience of growing up in a common educational framework is having. Whether between-group differences will be eroded will, though, depend on the experience of current and future generations of school leavers. Modood compared the qualifications of those born in Britain or who moved to Britain as children with those who came to Britain as adults.[39] He demonstrated that for Caribbeans there had been a dramatic inter-generational improvement in qualifications. The proportion of Indians without qualifications also reduced substantially compared to the migrant generation, though not as dramatically as for the Caribbeans. Second generation African Asians had enhanced their already high level of qualifications, such that twice as many 25–44-year-old as white people in this age range had degrees. Only the Chinese came near the levels of qualification of this group, and there the small sample size requires caution in use of the figures. Pakistanis showed some improvement in qualifications over the migrant generation, though they still fell a long way behind all other groups except the Bangladeshis, whose second -generation educational achievement showed no improvement over the qualifications levels of the migrants. As this group is the most recent to have migrated these results may be influenced by the fact that the definition of second generation includes those who moved to Britain at up to the age of 15. The fairly small sample size indicates that if birth in Britain had been the sole criterion there would have been insufficient numbers on the basis of which to judge. Nevertheless, there is a suggestion that the highly concentrated and impoverished experience of the Bangladeshis, combined with lack of fluency in English among some mothers, may not be enabling their children to improve their qualifications and therefore improve the possibilities for their outcomes. These findings suggest that passing through the British school system has enabled groups to improve the levels of their qualifications compared to the migrant generation. At the same time, it also illustrates that, on the whole, the higher the overall levels of qualification in the group the greater the gain is, with the exception of the Caribbean group, where the pattern may be influenced by the timing of migration and the greater number who have therefore been born in Britain. It is also, of course, the case that qualifications only capture one part of the social and cultural capital that groups bring with them and which they can pass onto their children, as was indicated in the discussion of groups' immigration history.

Another way of thinking about education and its implications for groups' futures is to compare the educational achievement among those currently leaving school or currently entering the job market. This will also give some indication of what to look forward to in the future.

Trends in attainment at compulsory school leaving age reflect the wider trends outlined above, as Figure 5.3 shows. Thus the proportion gaining five or more GCSEs at A* to C grades doubled for Indian children between 1988 and 1997 and more than doubled for Bangladeshis. Nevertheless, this did not mean a reduction in the between-group gaps across the board. The gap between Pakistani and white children increased, as did that between black groups and white groups. Thus, increasing absolute success for some groups was paralleled by increasing relative disadvantage. Comparison between 1995 and 1997, though, suggests that the gaps may now be reducing, with the exception of increasing Indian success.

Figure 5.3

Proportion of schoolchildren achieving five or more GCSEs grades A* to C by ethnic group, 1988 and 1997

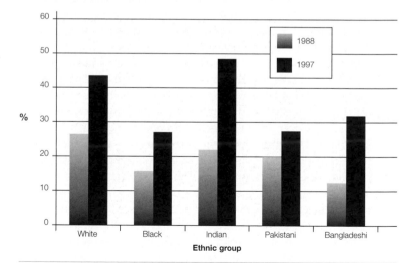

Source: D Gillborn and H S Mirza, *Educational Inequality: mapping race, class and gender*, OFSTED, November 2000, Figure 2

Evidence about qualifications at age 18 suggests that some of the differences in achievement are made up for by that age. The *Youth Cohort Study* is the best source for this information, though unfortunately it has insufficient numbers to provided reliable estimates for black groups. It does enable the picture for Indians and for Pakistanis and Bangladeshis relative to the whole of their cohort to be identified. The results for 2000 indicate that among 18-year-olds the picture is not straightforward, as is illustrated in Figure 5.4. While Indians are clearly the most highly qualified of the groups considered at this age, Pakistanis and Bangladeshis are under-represented both in relation to level three qualifications but also have a smaller proportion than the cohort as a whole with limited (below level 2) qualifications. By age 18 this group has improved its level of qualifications relative to its achievement at 16. This can, in part, be explained by higher staying-on rates in full-time education among all minority groups relative to the population as a whole.

There is substantial evidence that some minority group members remain in education for longer periods, not just gaining higher qualifica-

Figure 5.4

Highest qualification at age 18 by ethnic group, 2000

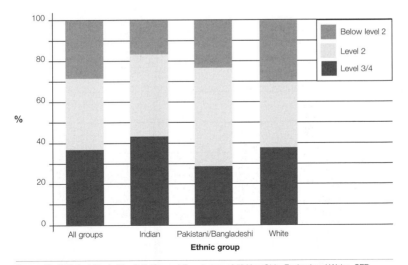

Source: *Youth Cohort Study: The Activities and Experiences of 18 Year Olds: England and Wales*, SFR 03/2001, Table E

tions – though that would seem to be the case for Chinese and to a lesser extent Indian young people – but also 'catching up' to compensate for underachievement during school years. Another possible reason for staying on is awareness of the difficult conditions ahead: 'an expectation of discrimination in the labour market may encourage some ethnic minority young people to stay longer in education than they would otherwise do with the aim of increasing their competitiveness in the labour market.'[40] At age 18, as Figure 5.5 illustrates, full-time education is the main activity of three-quarters of Indians and 70 per cent of Pakistanis and Bangladeshis, compared with a rate of 42 per cent in the population as a whole. The corollary of this is that employment rates among these two minority groups is much lower than in the population, but whether this is cause or effect is harder to determine.

Thus gaps in achievement between groups at ages 16 or 18 will not *necessarily* mean a poorer educational profile for those who were at a disadvantage up to school leaving age. And the extension of education does

Figure 5.5

Main activity at age 18 by ethnic group, 2000

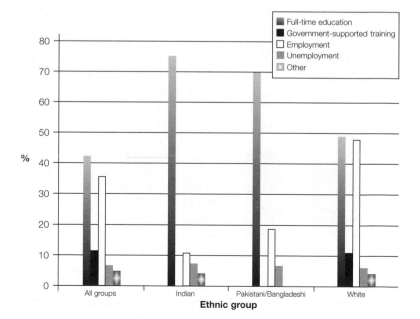

not simply apply to those staying on at 16 and beyond. In addition, some minority group members are more likely to attend university as mature students rather than straight from school, either due to acquiring qualifications and further qualifications later or, as seems to be more common with Caribbean women, following a period of employment. Thus, we find that, in 1997, while 35 per cent of all 16–24 year-olds were in full-time education, nearly 70 per cent of Chinese young people were in full-time education between these ages. The corresponding figures were 58 per cent of Indians, 47 per cent of those from black groups and 45 per cent of Pakistanis and Bangladeshis.[41] Nevertheless, educational qualifications achieved later seem to be less highly valued by employers, with older graduates experiencing higher unemployment rates than younger ones, and the length of time spent achieving a qualification has a disturbing positive association with unemployment.[42] Those who attempt to compensate for discrimination and disadvantage through improving their qualifications may find themselves in the position of facing discrimination on the basis of their mature student position.

The impact of social class

An important issue in understanding the differences in minority ethnic group educational achievement is the continuing impact of social class. Social class impacts on outcomes across ethnic groups and the continuing salience of social class to educational outcomes is the source of much academic discussion as well as numerous policy initiatives. Just as increasing educational achievement across all ethnic groups has been accompanied by some widening in the achievement gap between groups, so the increasing level of educational achievement generally has been accompanied by some widening in the gap between groups of low and high achievers according to social class background.[43]

Ethnic differences among pre-school age children can largely be explained by differences in their parents' occupational and educational positions.[44] However, the impact of social class on ethnic outcomes within school is hard to calculate without information that connects social class and outcome at the level of individual pupils. In addition, what occurs within schools in relation to minority group pupils and the impact of school practices on outcomes is hard to generalise about given the diversity of experiences and outcomes in different local education authorities, combined with somewhat partial ethnic monitoring of

pupils. However, a number of studies suggest that schools impact neg-
atively on the achievement of pupils from black groups: such pupils
enter school in a relatively strong baseline position, but leave school
achieving below the average.[45] Studies have implicated low teacher
expectations, the impact of labelling, and harsh disciplinary treatment.[46]
The Commission for Racial Equality in 1992 also drew attention to the
negative impacts of streaming, where pupils from South Asian groups
were allocated to sets below their ability with a consequent impact on
their outcomes.[47]

One area that has been systematically monitored since a
Commission for Racial Equality investigation first drew attention to it in
1985 in an investigation of Birmingham schools is the higher rates of
exclusion experienced by black pupils. Considerable recent attention to
the issue has come not just from within the Department for Education and
Skills, but also from the Social Exclusion Unit; exclusions of black pupils
have since declined.[48] School exclusion has now become less of a focus
within government, which may lead to rates rising again, with consequences for Caribbean and black African pupils who are still more likely to
be excluded from school than other ethnic groups. For the small number
of individuals who are excluded, the consequences for subsequent life-
chances can be bleak.[49] Moreover, while the numbers of exclusions, even
among Caribbeans, is too small to have a substantial direct impact on the
group as a whole, rates of exclusion may well represent the extreme point
of a wider issue of conflict and disciplinary problems.

Thus, even the amount of explanation that is provided by educational achievement for differences in labour market experience and poverty may not be *simply* an educational effect, or even a result of the
connection between social class and educational outcome. Rather, the
contribution of poorer educational results to poorer outcomes for some
groups may themselves stem from an ethnic effect or ethnic penalty operating at the school level. This is worth bearing in mind in the discussion
below of the ethnic penalty, which illustrates that there are effects of ethnicity *even when* controlling for, and therefore treating as neutral, such factors as educational achievement.

So are those young people who gain the same levels of qualification
as each other as likely as each other to move into employment? Does
educational level explain for today's school and university leavers, even if
not for the minority groups as a whole, the different patterns of youth
employment and unemployment? The answer is that it is insufficient.
Educational attainment on its own accounts for only 12 per cent of differ-

ences in unemployment rates between ethnic groups.[50] It is clear that educational qualifications do not translate into equal possibilities for all who hold them: age of attainment impacts on the power of qualifications; for those with degrees, the class of the degree is also relevant; and social class background remains important.

Studies have repeatedly reported an association between social class origins and destinations. While some of this effect is mediated through educational achievement, with the consequences discussed above, social class origin would also appear to affect final class position and lifetime income levels regardless of educational success.[51] The different social class positions of minority groups can therefore be anticipated to have an impact on their labour market position, which might explain some of the lack of direct relationship between qualification level and labour market outcome, in particular, for the more highly qualified groups. Thus, smaller proportions of graduates from all minority groups and across both sexes, with the exception of Caribbean women, succeed in gaining access to the 'service class' than white graduates.[52] However, the picture is further complicated by the fact that the occupational level of older generations may not accurately reflect their inherent social class position in terms of their social and cultural capital. Thus the apparent 'success', even if not a success that is effective at the highest levels, of the Indian and, in particular, the African Asian groups, can be interpreted as a reassertion of the underlying social class position rather than an upward mobility.[53]

In the following final section of this chapter the role of discrimination in contributing to poorer labour market outcomes among minorities is considered. As Sly and others comment: 'Overall, it does not appear that variation in age profiles and qualifications held across ethnic groups explains much of the large overall differences in unemployment rates.'[54] So, if education and demography cannot fully explain the greater disadvantage of minority ethnic groups in employment with its consequences for poverty, the obvious factor to consider is the role of discrimination.

Discrimination in employment

There have been two ways of ascertaining discrimination in the labour market: the first is to attempt directly to assess it through measuring people's responses to particular questions or their judgement of, say, job applications from members of different minority groups. It is important, moreover, to distinguish between measures which demonstrate discrimination occurring and evidence of beliefs that discrimination occurs or has occurred. Such beliefs are regularly cited as evidence of discrimination, but they cannot demonstrate the extent of discrimination or whether its levels have altered over time.

The other way of assessing the extent of discrimination on an outcome is to assume that discrimination is what is left when all other factors have been accounted for. For example, if there is a difference in unemployment rate once the factors that have been discussed above (age, educational level, region, gender, etc.) have been controlled for, then it is assumed that the remaining difference can be put down to discrimination, even if it is not clear in so doing exactly where or how it is operating. There is also a more cautious version of this approach, which assumes that discrimination cannot be discounted as long as that gap remains. As Pathak expresses it in relation to explanations of differential employment experience: 'After allowing for differences in personal characteristics, large differences in employment rates between white and minority ethnic men remain. This means discrimination by employers cannot be ruled out as a key factor'.[55]

Take first the perceptions of, and beliefs about, discrimination. While these may not give us categorical evidence on actual practices of discrimination they can nevertheless be informative in indicating how people experience the labour market (and society as a whole) and for the assessment of the obstacles faced that it provides. Perception of difficulties in gaining employment may also influence action. While, as discussed above, there is no evidence that greater susceptibility to long-term unemployment affects attachment to the labour market, those who face difficulties in gaining access to areas of work may adopt alternative work strategies. They may take up self-employment, or pursue more and higher educational qualifications to compensate for the effects of discrimination; they may seek work in sectors that are seen as more 'accessible' or less discriminatory. Women from backgrounds that strongly endorse more traditional patterns of behaviour of staying at home and looking after family may find this option more appealing if the labour market is perceived as unreceptive. And it is those very women who are or are perceived as being more culturally conforming, Muslim women who wear the *hijab* for example, who may experience the greatest levels of stereotyping and resistance to them as employees.[56] Perceptions, then, are important in helping to understand other aspects of the structure of the labour market.

There is evidence of a widespread belief that discrimination in employment against individuals from minority ethnic groups is a feature of the British labour market. In 1993, Modood found that a vast majority of all groups considered that at least some employers discriminated, with 90 per cent of economically active white respondents believing this to be the case and between 60 and 95 per cent of minority groups supporting this belief.[57] However, the relationship between beliefs and actual occurrence or prevalence is hard to assess. More valuable evidence may come from people's own reports of experience of discrimination. Of those ever economically active, 28 per cent of Caribbeans, 19 per cent of African Asians and 15 per cent of Indians, but only 7 per cent of Chinese and 5 per cent of Bangladeshis considered that they had been discriminated against in a job application. Here again, it is rarely possible for an applicant to know that they have been discriminated against, and what are being measured are perceptions, which may vary with factors other than actual discriminatory practice. The different rates of perceived employment discrimination *may*, nevertheless, reflect the different responses to groups: there has been, according to some sources, a persistent stereotype among employers that regards Caribbeans as 'lazy' or 'slow'.[58] Alternatively, different perceptions of the extent of discrimination may reflect differences in the occupational sectors in which the different groups tend to be concentrated and, related to this, they may reflect the degree of labour market segmentation experienced by the different groups. A highly segregated market is unlikely to be as discriminatory within each segment. Thus, more discrimination may reflect a potentially more open market, or more opportunities for direct competition.[59] Such inferences, remain, however, somewhat speculative.

Additionally, what is understood by 'discrimination' may affect responses. Those who incorporate in their understanding the notion of indirect as well as direct discrimination may be more likely to report experience of discrimination, since it is potentially easier to detect organisational failings or particular recruitment processes that disadvantage members of particular minority groups than it is to observe clearly a process of direct discrimination. A related issue is the increase in the number of complaints of discrimination to the Commission for Racial Equality (CRE): while this may reflect an increase in discrimination, it may also reflect greater confidence in the ability to complain, or the greater relevance of discrimination higher up the occupational hierarchy.

If there are limits, then, to the amount that respondents' beliefs can tell us about the labour market, what direct evidence is there of employer discrimination?

The work of the CRE has been crucial in highlighting examples of direct and indirect discrimination in employment since it came into being in 1976. It has investigated both individual companies and conducted more general investigations into particular sectors or geographical areas.[60] In December 2000 it issued its first formal notice under the new race relations legislation against an employer – Hackney Council –where discrimination had been found to be widespread in an investigation of 1997, alongside an equally pernicious failure to do anything about it.[61] The CRE and studies emanating from other sources have also revealed direct employer discrimination through testing comparable job applications from applicants of different ethnicity, or where written details or telephone requests imply minority group membership. For example, Brown and Gay identified substantial levels of employer discrimination by using a system of putting three comparable applicants – one white, one of Asian origin and one Caribbean – forward for a range of jobs in three cities, using a range of approaches.[62] Such studies made a clear case for the prevalence of employer discrimination across the last few decades.[63] The evidence from the 1970s to the 1990s suggested that around a third of employers practice such direct discrimination.[64] And in 1996 the CRE tested for employer discrimination in the North of England and Scotland, finding substantial evidence of discrimination in relation to Asian and Afro-Caribbean applicants.[65] Complaints lodged with industrial tribunals and successful hearings can also give an indication of discrimination by employers, both direct and indirect. It should be noted here that relatively few complaints reach the stage of tribunals. However, a TUC hotline provided evidence of an underlying volume of discrimination and racism at work. Nearly 90 calls a day to the hotline over the course of a week outlined experiences ranging from daily racist abuse, to not being informed about promotion opportunities, to having belongings damaged or experiencing violence, to being refused references. They also highlighted a high degree of complacency at managerial level.[66] These experiences revealed not only the existence of direct and indirect discrimination within the workplace, but also the issue of 'institutional racism', where a culture of antagonistic behaviour was accompanied by the failure of managers to take responsibility for it or action against it.

Given the difficulty of accurately assessing discrimination in employment, as well as the ethical considerations attached to 'test' applications,[67] discrimination is commonly taken to be evidenced by the differentials in employment outcomes themselves.[68] This both enables a measure of extent and impact to be taken and also illustrates differences in experience, which then beg further explanation.

Quantitative studies have argued that discrimination is indicated if analysis shows that when characteristics are controlled for (and thus like is compared with like) differences in outcome exist. It is left open whether it is direct or indirect discrimination that is implied, though it tends to be assumed that it is direct discrimination. As the evidence of this chapter has shown, while there are many possible factors accounting for excess poverty among minority groups, each constellation of factors that affects each different group remains insufficient to explain in full the particular patterns of poverty experienced by these groups. For many, the existence of deficits that remain to be explained are clear evidence of discrimination. For example, Blackaby and others found that taking into account levels of human capital, residential area, employment sector, and looking only at the cohort which was born in Britain could only explain a fifth of the observed employment differentials. Their conclusion was that ethnic minorities faced persistent discrimination, which was having no less of an impact in the 1990s than in the 1970s and was affecting the British-born generation as much as the migrant generation.[69] They expand the point by expressing the concern that the stress on qualifications, and regional and sectoral distributions, may not only obscure but also exacerbate this primary issue of discrimination. They state that 'such generalisations about attributes of the ethnic minority populations can reinforce stereotyping, which may result in these populations being excluded from the most remunerative jobs and excuse government from taking appropriate policy initiatives in this area.'[70]

An alternative, and more circumspect, version of the consideration that any gap left when other factors have been accounted for is the notion of the 'ethnic penalty', as investigated by Heath and McMahon. They use the expression ethnic penalty:

> 'to refer to all the sources of disadvantage that might lead an ethnic [minority] group to fare less well in the labour market than do similarly qualified whites. In other words, it is a broader concept than that of discrimination, although discrimination is likely to be a major component of the ethnic penalty.'[71]

Thus, while absolute outcomes may be very different for different groups, and while the strength of the ethnic penalty may vary between groups, all non-white groups suffer an additional penalty that is taken to relate to their

minority ethnic status. After analysing Census data on both first generation minority groups and those born in Britain, Heath and McMahon determine that despite substantial differences between groups, both
generations suffer an equivalent ethnic penalty. They conclude that 'the
range in sizes of the ethnic penalties for different minorities and for different competitions suggests that quite complex explanations will also be
required for them. Both direct discrimination and cultural differences will
surely play a part in explaining our findings.'[72] While such ethnic penalties
will prevent those more qualified from reaching the highest positions, for
those already in a less privileged position it may increase the probability of
a fall into poverty. The idea of the ethnic penalty has been criticised for
homogenising the experience of minority groups despite the very evidence
that the ethnic penalty is weaker or stronger for some groups.[73]
Nevertheless, that is to separate it out from the factors, especially social
class position, which make the absolute experience of different groups so
different. It is perhaps not so useful to think in terms of an ethnic penalty
as operating over and above the other characteristics which affect an individual's outcome (such as those considered in this chapter). Instead, the
ethnic penalty should be seen as inseparable from the other characteristics which combine to lead to an excess of poverty for certain minority
groups. Thus the size and impact of the penalty will itself alter with the particular context of the individual or group.

Overall then, even when the impact of associated factors is taken
into account, there still remains an effect of ethnicity which cannot be
reduced to any of the proposed structural explanations. As Modood put
it: 'ethnic minorities have to be not just as good as but better than their
white competitors to get the job.'[74]

Clearly, part of what makes a minority group categorisation meaningful is the recognition that it is in part created by processes of allocation
and discrimination. To a certain extent, the very fact that ethnic minorities
are distinguished, that different patterns of experience can be identified
and that a book like this exists presuppose the existence of discrimination
as at least one contributory factor in that experience. It is also important
to recognise, as this chapter has indicated, that discrimination, either past
or ongoing, is implicated in many of the 'structural' factors that have been
considered, such as residential and occupational concentration and segregation and educational outcomes, as well as possibly in supposedly
'cultural' factors, discussed in the last chapter, such as high rates of lone
parenthood among Caribbean women and low economic activity rates
among Pakistani and Bangladeshi women.

If, then, ethnic minorities face excess poverty in large part through not only low insufficient earnings but also extreme rates of unemployment, what is it about unemployment, or worklessness more generally, that means that it causes poverty? And is the poverty of unemployment greater for minority ethnic groups than it is for the population as a whole? These are the questions that are considered in Chapter 6.

Notes

1 V Robinson, 'The Indians: onward and upward' in C Peach (ed), *Ethnicity in the 1991 Census: Volume Two: the ethnic minority populations of Great Britain*, HMSO, 1996

2 R Dorsett, *Ethnic Minorities in the Inner City*, The Policy Press, 1998

3 R Ballard, 'The Pakistanis: stability and introspection' in C Peach (ed), *Ethnicity in the 1991 Census: Volume Two: the ethnic minority populations of Great Britain*, HMSO, 1996

4 J Eade, T Vamplew and C Peach, 'The Bangladeshis: the encapsulated community', in C Peach (ed), *Ethnicity in the 1991 Census: Volume Two: the ethnic minority populations of Great Britain*, HMSO, 1996, p150. Peach has tried to estimate the numbers of 'Bangladeshis' across the decades from 1961.

5 See note 4

6 See note 4; A Scott, D Pearce and P Goldblatt, 'The Sizes and Characteristics of the Minority Ethnic Populations of Great Britain – Latest Estimates', *Population Trends*, Office for National Statistics, Autumn 2001

7 T Phillips and M Phillips, *Windrush*, Harper Collins, 1999; see also B Parekh, *The Future of Multi-Ethnic Britain* (The Parekh Report), Profile Books, 2000, p104

8 C Peach, 'Black Caribbeans: class, gender and geography' in *Ethnicity in the 1991 Census: Volume Two: the ethnic minority populations of Great Britain*, HMSO, 1996

9 P Daley, 'Black Africans: students who stayed' in C Peach (ed), *Ethnicity in the 1991 Census: Volume Two: the ethnic minority populations of Great Britain*, HMSO, 1996, pp44 and 49

10 See note 6, p10

11 Y Cheng, 'The Chinese: upwardly mobile' in C Peach, *Ethnicity in the 1991 Census: Volume Two: the ethnic minority populations of Great Britain*, HMSO, 1996

12 F Edholm, H Roberts and J Sayer, *Vietnamese Refugees in Britain*, Commission for Racial Equality, 1983

13 P Iganski and G Payne, 'Socio-economic Restructuring and Employment: the case of minority ethnic groups', *The British Journal of Sociology*, 50, 1999

14 See note 11

15 See note 4

16 See note 3

17 See note 8

18 See note 1

19 B Twomey, 'Labour Market Participation of Ethnic Groups', *Labour Market Trends*, January 2001

20 S Pathak, *Race Research for the Future*, DfEE Research Topic Paper RTP01, March 2000, p12

21 D Wilkinson 'Who Are the Low Paid?' *Labour Market Trends*, December 1998, p620

22 Low Pay Commission, *The National Minimum Wage*, First Report, Cm3976, June 1998, pp34 and 38-39.

23 A Felstead and N Jewson, with J Goodwin, *Homeworkers in Britain*, DTI and DfEE, 1996

24 D H Blackby, D G Leslie, P D Murphy and N C O'Leary, 'White/Ethnic Minority Earnings and Employment Differentials in Britain: evidence from the LFS', *Oxford Economic Papers* 54, 2002

25 *Labour Force Survey Historical Supplement: 1984-2000*, National Statistics, 2000. The rate for men from non-manual occupations was 2.9 per cent compared to 6.8 per cent for those from manual occupations; while for women the rates were 2.6 per cent and 5.1 per cent respectively. For both sexes the rates were 2.7 per cent and 6.2 per cent.

26 See note 19, pp609-610

27 D Owen, B Reza, A Green, M Maguire and J Pitcher, 'Patterns of Labour Market Participation in Ethnic Minority Groups', *Labour Market Trends*, November 2000, p506

28 A Dale, E Fieldhouse, N Shaheen and V Kalra, 'The Labour Market Prospects for Pakistani and Bangladeshi Women', *Work, Employment and Society* 16.1, 2002

29 F Sly, T Thair, A Risdon, 'Trends in the Labour Market Participation of Ethnic Groups', *Labour Market Trends*, December 1999, p633

30 R Berthoud, *Young Caribbean Men and the Labour Market: a comparison with other ethnic groups*, Joseph Rowntree Foundation, 1999

31 See note 27, p509

32 See note 27, p509

33 See, in this light, the comments from young female respondents, note 28.

34 J M Thomas, 'Who Feels It Knows It: work attitudes and excess non-white unemployment in the UK', *Ethnic and Racial Studies* 21, 1998

35 The exit rates for black groups were not significantly different from white

groups whether attitudes were or were not taken into account, though the data suggested that they also had a greater attachment to the labour market than their white peers.

36 T Modood, 'Qualifications and English Language' in T Modood, R Berthoud *et al*, *Ethnic Minorities in Britain: diversity and disadvantage*, Policy Studies Institute, 1997

37 The estimate for higher qualifications for Bangladeshis would appear to be low here by comparison with note 36, Table 3.5, p65, and with the 1991 Census.

38 G Smith, 'Schools' in A H Halsey and J Webb (eds), *Twentieth Century British Social Trends*, Macmillan, 2000

39 See note 36

40 See note 20, p8

41 See note 19, Table 7, p 610

42 See note 20, pp9, 11

43 See note 36, p18

44 See note 20, p3

45 See note 36, p17

46 D Gillborn and C Gipps, *Recent Research on the Achievements of Ethnic Minority Pupils*, OFSTED, 1996, pp54-57

47 Commission for Racial Equality, *Set to Fail: setting and banding in secondary schools*, CRE, 1992; see also D Gillborn and D Youdell, *Rationing Education: policy, practice, reform and equity*, Open University Press, 2000, for a description of the way allocations to GCSE tiers disadvantage Caribbean pupils in a similar way.

48 Social Exclusion Unit, *Truancy and School Exclusion*, May 1998

48 Department for Education and Skills, *Permanent Exclusions from Schools, England 1999/2000*, SFR 32/2001, July 2001

50 See note 24

51 A Heath and C Payne, 'Social Mobility' in A H Halsey and J Webb (eds), *Twentieth Century British Social Trends*, Macmillan, 2000

52 See note 51, Table 10

53 T Modood 'Employment' in T Modood, R Berthoud *et al*, *Ethnic Minorities in Britain: diversity and disadvantage*, Policy Studies Institute, 1997

54 See note 29, p633

55 See note 20, p2

56 See note 28, p22

57 See note 53, p130

58 See note 53, p149

59 See note 53

60 Examples of general investigations from the 1980s and 1990s are Commission

for Racial Equality, *A Study of Employment in Kirklees*, 1984; Commission for Racial Equality, *Employers in Cardiff*, 1991; Commission for Racial Equality, *Working in Hotels: recruitment and selection*, 1991

61 See http://www.cre.gov.uk/media/nr_arch/nr001205.html, for the press release concerning this non-discrimination notice.

62 C Brown and P Gay, *Racial Discrimination: 17 years after the Act*, Policy Studies Institute, 1985

63 B Parekh, *The Future of Multi-Ethnic Britain*, (The Parekh Report), Profile Books, 2000, p337-338; and note 53

64 See note 53, p132

65 Commission for Racial Equality, *We Regret to Inform You: testing for racial discrimination in youth employment in the North of England and Scotland*, 1996

66 TUC, *Exposing Racism at Work*, July 2000

67 M Banton, 'The Ethics of Practice Testing', *New Community* 23.3, 1997

68 For an example of this approach see, for example, TUC, *Black and Excluded: black and Asian workers in the 1990s*, 1999, which cites as discrimination the evidence from employment differentials.

69 See for example, note 24, pp294-295

70 See note 24, p294

71 A Heath and D McMahon, 'Educational and Occupational Attainments: the impact of ethnic origins' in V Karn (ed), *Ethnicity in the 1991 Census: Volume Four: employment, education and housing among the ethnic minority populations of Britain*, p91

72 See note 71, p109

73 See note 53, p146

74 See note 53, p145

Six

The experience of social security

Chapter 5 explored the different elements that contribute to disadvantage in the labour market with its consequences for the poverty of minority ethnic groups. In this chapter, the issue of why it is that unemployment and labour market disadvantage result in poverty is taken up by considering ethnic minority groups' experience of social security.[1]

For those unemployed or otherwise economically inactive, the state provides social security support through a mixture of benefits. While these benefits do not directly differentiate according to ethnic group, there are a number of ways in which the welfare benefits system may contribute to or exacerbate the experience of poverty among members of some minority ethnic groups. First, there is the issue that the rates of use of means-tested benefits are higher among minority groups. The call on means-tested rather than contributory benefits not only has financial implications, it also affects the relationship between the claimant and benefits agencies, since means-tested benefits tend to be more stringently 'policed' than other benefits. The administration of checks on eligibility or the way the rules are interpreted may affect the amount of benefit received, as well as being a potentially humiliating experience. On the other hand, the delivery of the New Deals, intended to move people off income-based jobseeker's allowance and into work may result in different outcomes for members of different ethnic groups. The links made between immigration and social security may further affect benefit payment or, in the case of asylum seekers, the amount of benefit. Additionally, there are a number of reasons why those eligible for benefit may not claim their entitlement, and this can vary with ethnic group for a number of reasons. This chapter explores all these aspects of the relationship between minority groups and social security in order to illuminate how the position of worklessness can be particularly punitive for some minority ethnic groups.

Means-tested benefits

First, then, there is the differential probability of receipt of means-tested benefits rather than national insurance benefits. The relevance of means-tested benefits as an indicator of poverty was discussed in Chapter 2 and the differential use of means-tested benefits by ethnic group was shown in Chapter 3, Table 3.8, and is illustrated again, here, in Figure 6.1.

Figure 6.1

Receipt of means-tested benefits among minority ethnic groups

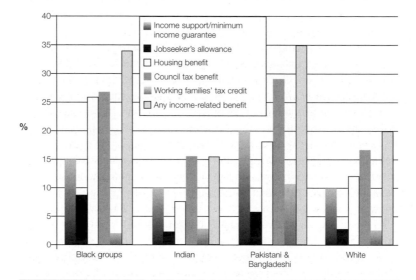

Source: Adapted from Department for Work and Pensions, *Family Resources Survey Great Britain 2000-01*, 2002, Table 3.17

Those for whom worklessness or low pay results in receipt of a means-tested benefit – in particular income support or its equivalent for those seeking work, income-based jobseeker's allowance – are more likely to suffer poverty than those who are not dependent on means-tested support. This is because the rationale of income support is that it must not seem like a 'desirable' option, that it must be kept below levels at which people could support themselves through employment, and that it should only form a last recourse.[2] In Chapter 2 the rates of income support were illustrated. Means-tested benefits also incorporate an assets threshold, such that, for income support savings must not exceed £3,000 to avoid reduction in benefit and must not exceed £8,000 for any benefit to be obtained. For housing and council tax benefits the relevant amounts are savings lower than £8,000 for no reduction in benefit and no greater than £16,000 to be eligible for any benefit. Thus the receipt of income support and housing or council tax benefits is only an option for those with limited savings – or only becomes an option once 'excess' savings have been used. Thus, those on income support have, by definition, few resources available to them should there be an emergency or a need for a renewal of some essential household item, leading to material deprivation if benefit receipt persists. For such emergencies there is the possibility of application to the social fund, but that involves loan repayments being deducted from benefit and the refusal rate for grants is high; and there are also indications that some groups do not resort to the social fund.[3]

There are a number of reasons for the greater use of means-tested benefits among some minority ethnic groups. First there are issues of demography. As discussed in Chapter 4, the population profile of minority groups is younger than that of the population as a whole. This is particularly the case with the Pakistani and Bangladeshi groups. Those who are younger are less likely to have built up national insurance contributions through a lifetime's employment. They are more likely to have dependent children – and Chapter 4 also illustrated the large proportions of Pakistani and Bangladeshi families with dependent children – which will increase the probability of eligibility for working families' tax credit, as will the low pay issues discussed in Chapter 5. Family *structure* is also relevant. Even though Caribbean lone parents are more likely to work than lone parents from other groups, nevertheless half of them are still reliant on income support; and the high proportion of Caribbean lone parents, therefore, has implications for the use of means-tested benefits among this group.[4] On the other hand, the greater preponderance of large families among Pakistanis and Bangladeshis, combined with an unaccommodating labour market and problems of low pay, may push such families towards receipt of income support or income-based jobseeker's allowance.

The higher prevalence of unemployment, which was illustrated in Chapter 5, leads to greater use of means-tested benefits. While contribution-based jobseeker's allowance does exist, it only lasts for six months. For those unemployed for longer – and greater durations of unemployment particularly affect Pakistani and Bangladeshi men[5] – use of the contribution-based benefit ceases to be an option. In addition, many may not have built up sufficient contributions in the first place. Younger people, who, as we saw, were particularly at risk of unemployment, may simply not have had the opportunity to build up national insurance credits. This will also be a problem for those whose income falls below the national insurance threshold.

For those who have no or few qualifications, the prospects for young people for employment on leaving full-time education are increasingly problematic. On the other hand, benefits for this age group are more restricted than for those at older ages or those who have gained national insurance credits. For this group, as for those who are long-term unemployed, the New Deal may offer a way into paid work. However, access to the service may be influenced by an observed reluctance to transfer those from minority ethnic groups in receipt of income support to jobseeker's allowance, which would render them eligible for the New Deal programme. There is also the issue of the effectiveness of the New Deal itself. Evaluation of the New Deal for young people suggests that it is having a positive, if modest, effect and has increased the rate at which young men enter jobs from unemployment.[6] Evidence on the New Deal for long-term unemployed is not so clear-cut; while evaluations for the other New Deals is not currently available.

Furthermore, there is question of the extent to which the New Deal works for ethnic minorities in particular.[7] There are certainly a substantial number of minority group members involved in the New Deal, but they appear to follow rather different pathways out of it. By January 2000, 18 per cent of those on the New Deal were from a minority ethnic group. The proportions leaving for an unknown destination among all minority groups were higher than among white groups. Among those that were known, it was observed that only 17 per cent of black Africans entered unsubsidised employment compared with 26 per cent for the white group and the highest proportion, 30 per cent, among the Indian group.[8] Figures from a year later, December 2001, show that 15 per cent of those on the New Deal for Young People were from a minority group, about 3 per cent being Pakistanis, around 5 per cent being from black groups and with Indians making up around 2 per cent.[9] Again, the pathways through and out of the programme would appear to differ by ethnic group. Indians, were, by 2001, over-represented in moves into employment and Bangladeshis were most likely to take up the voluntary sector option, with black Africans more likely to take up further education and training. However, many minority group destinations were not recorded, and these findings need to be treated with some caution.

For older people, full state pension entitlement may not have been accrued. This could be due to timing of migration, resulting in an incomplete contributions record. The contributions record could also be affected by extended visits abroad to the country of origin often caused by the illness or death of a relative.[10] Even for those who do gain entitlement to the basic state pension, the rate of this falls below the minimum income guarantee for those without additional resources. Low pay and restricted occupational options during their working life render older minority group members less likely to be in receipt of an occupational or private pension. And Chapter 3 illustrated how most minority groups were less likely to have acquired assets over their lifetime.[11]

There is evidence that family credit was more difficult to claim successfully for those who were self-employed.[12] This problem may well also apply to its successor, working families' tax credit, and members of some ethnic groups are much more likely to be self-employed than others. In 1999/00 a quarter of Pakistani men were self-employed with high rates of 21 per cent and 19 per cent among Chinese and Indians respectively.[13] This compares with 15 per cent among white men. For those with children, then, the insecurity (and often low income) of self-employment may be accompanied by difficulties in gaining additional support from benefits.

In addition, means-testing may affect groups differently. The value of income support varies with the characteristics of the family. For example, the minimum income guarantee for pensioners is set at a higher level than the standard single and couple rates. A study from 1998/99 illustrated that income support provides a lower proportion of the needs of large families compared with small families, assessed on the basis of budget standards work.[14] If benefit is being used for long-term support where a household has economically inactive adults, for example, resources will be drained over time and the deprivation and social exclusion will increase.

Administration and delivery

There are also issues concerning the administration and delivery of benefits. A number of studies have highlighted the obstacles potential claimants may face in attempting to access benefits. Such obstacles occur in the rules that govern benefits, in the way they are delivered, and in the treatment and the interpretation of the rules. Bloch has identified a number of ways in which benefit rules themselves can disadvantage certain minority group members.[15] Residence requirements can affect those who have spent or spend substantial periods of time abroad. Where people have geographically distant ties, they may choose or be obliged to spend substantial periods away from Britain, a pattern that has been particularly noted for South Asian groups. There may also be problems in the interpretation and application of the notorious 'habitual residence test'. This provision requires a judgement about whether someone is 'habitually resident' and there is substantial evidence to show that it tends to be operated inappropriately, and that the recourse to it is a result of racist stereotyping and assumptions.[16] As NACAB put it in 1996, the 'habitual residence test has created a space where prejudices and unexamined assumptions concerning race and culture can appear legitimate.'[17]

Extended visits to the country of origin and the extent of accumulation of assets also draw attention to the related issue of practices of income transfers which extend beyond the boundaries of the immediate family and beyond national borders. The issue of money being sent to family overseas was highlighted in Chapter 3. The Department for Work and Pensions, however, does not acknowledge the claims of family who are abroad, even if it is delays in immigration processes which are keeping them there. On the other hand, it does recognise assets that are held abroad for the purposes of assessing whether capital exceeds the limits. In their study in the mid-1980s, Gordon and Newnham found that unnecessary verification of the value of assets abroad, which clearly fell below the capital limits could be used to delay or deny benefit. In addition, it has been found that where benefits have been in payment but the claimant is absent for a period the family may not claim the support due.[18]

There may also be differential requests for documentary evidence required to support a claim according to the ethnicity of the claimant, and problems with accepting or interpreting that evidence. Gordon and Newnham drew attention to unreasonable requests for passports, resulting on occasion in misinterpretation by the (then) DHSS officials of the stamps in them.[19] They also related that unreasonable evidence was sometimes sought to prove a 'genuine' marriage or the particular status of a marriage contracted in another country. More recently, the practice of requests for passports or other 'excessive demands for evidence' was again highlighted.[20] Such requests, if they cannot be met, may result in benefit being withheld and consequent hardship.

The interaction between the Home Office and the Department for Work and Pensions is also pertinent, both to eligibility for benefit and to the way it is delivered for some minority group members. In some cases, ability to claim benefit will be limited by immigration status or that of relatives. Since 1966 there has been the requirement that those seeking family reunification, that is, applying for dependants from abroad to join them, have no 'recourse to public funds' at the time of the application and for a year after the dependant(s) have joined them. 'Public funds' for these purposes means the means-tested benefits housing benefit, council tax benefit and income support/income-based jobseeker's allowance. Those who wish to apply for family to join them are thus discouraged from claiming benefits and may, therefore, have to subsist at inadequate levels of support. If they, or their dependants, should then claim before they have gained settlement it could imperil their status. Studies have also shown inappropriate communication between the Home Office and social security staff, whereby those delivering social security took on themselves to act as agents of immigration control in relation to claimants who applied to them.[21]

Recently, attention has been given to the experience of asylum seekers in relation to the benefit system as the result of the highly contentious, but now abandoned, use of vouchers in place of cash payments. Particular limitations on benefit claiming have long existed for those with ambiguous or unconfirmed status. On the one hand, asylum seekers are prohibited from working and thus obliged to be dependent upon the state. On the other hand, the claiming of benefits is perceived as problematic.

For this group, their immigration status has, in recent years, taken them out of the main social security system in relation to benefits. Financial support for refugees applying for asylum is now dealt with by the National Asylum Support Service (NASS) which provides a level of financial support that is lower than income support for adults, rendering them even more susceptible to poverty. Asylum seekers who are self-maintaining are also not eligible for the 'universal' child benefit. While the notorious vouchers by which support is provided were phased out in the autumn of 2002, the separate provision by NASS of restricted financial (and housing) support will continue.[22] The separation of one, peculiarly vulnerable, group from mainstream support serves both to compound their exclusion and to convey highly racialised messages about entitlement and eligibility. The provision (or refusal) of welfare thus becomes part of a system which responds to, enforces or acts as a means of control on formal status.[23] It may also act to control or discourage those who are perceived as being non-British, regardless of their status.

The permeation of social security provision by such racialised behaviours and assumptions and the ways it interacts with the claimant profile may mean that the process of dealing with claims and claimants is conducted in such a way that it puts off eligible claimants. Means-tested benefits already come with a stigma attached.[24] If that stigma is combined with assumptions relating to the ethnicity of the claimant the whole application procedure may become intolerable. As one Pakistani mother expressed it:

> 'There is no doubt that they don't look well on us people and that is why it takes so long to get an answer from them, or when it's late they take even longer. It's more difficult if you don't know the language or can't read or write English.'[25]

The stigma may be exacerbated, as mentioned here, by lack of fluency in English. It may also be exacerbated by perceptions about particular claimant groups. Lone parents are the subject of a highly stigmatising discourse in this country, partly as a result of their use of income support.[26] Caribbean lone parents who claim income support may therefore be subjected to stigmatising attitudes at a number of levels. The very fact that there are known to be relatively high proportions of Caribbean lone parents, compared to the proportions in other groups, may serve to exacerbate this.

One response to stigma may be to fail to claim entitlement. This takes us to the issue of take-up: the specific question of whether eligible minority group members are claiming their entitlement. While the higher rates of reliance upon means-tested benefits explored in Chapter 3 are one indication of poverty, there is evidence that it is some of those not in receipt of income support who are yet worse off.[27] This may be a consequence of failure to claim entitlement, which could occur for a number of reasons. The impact of stigma has been explored in a study by Law and others.[28] This study found that it was Chinese respondents who were particularly sensitive to the stigma of benefit claiming. The implication of this is that, despite the overall profile of the group as relatively successful, there may a small group of very poor Chinese who are not receiving benefit entitlement and who are insufficiently captured by existing data sources. Attitudes to stigma among Bangladeshi Muslims in the same study were less clear-cut. A number of the young men expressed reluctance to claim benefit. For example, one commented that:

'As a young person, I don't want to go on the dole, I don't think people would approve of a young person being on benefit when I could find a job. This is why I have decided not to claim benefit yet. I wouldn't claim unless I had absolutely no money to buy necessities.'[29]

However, for other respondents there was a sense that benefit had been earned or was an appropriate recourse of 'last resort', an attitude that can be seen to be also hinted at in the above quotation.

For some, problems of access to information can inhibit claiming, especially given the enormous complexity of the benefit system. Information in appropriate languages has been shown to be a problem in the past, but access to appropriate advice and guidance outside of the benefit offices themselves can also be an issue.[30] The Department for Work and Pensions now produces information in a range of languages both in paper form and on its website.[31] However, there may be a danger that emphasis on translation and information provision can obscure other issues, both those concerning the way information is accessed and the way that delivery issues, such as those discussed above, can impede effective claiming.[32] In relation to access, many local offices have in recent years developed liaison roles in order to take information and advice to communities. On the other hand, the tendency to reduce the numbers of local offices maintained can make benefits advice less accessible to those who do, or would, use them.

As this discussion has made clear, there is a clear need for research which will identify and clarify patterns of benefit take-up and non-take-up by ethnic group and for systematically investigate their causes, associations and impacts. While information and own language issues are both widely acknowledged and are being addressed, other factors which lead to the exclusion of claimants from benefit and their possible solutions require further attention. Such a research agenda was highlighted in 1991[33] and was reiterated in 2002.[34] In addition, there is a need to clarify the differential impact of benefit rules and rates on different minority ethnic groups. One element necessary for achieving these ends is the comprehensive monitoring of both benefit recipients and benefit applications.[35] The Department for Work and Pensions' race equality consultation document, produced under the requirements of the Race Relations Amendment Act 2000, notes the need to develop the monitoring of both its employees and its clients. The importance of pursuing these objectives, and the question of how readily this is likely to be achieved, is taken up further in the following and concluding chapter of this book, which considers issues of policy and areas for action.

35 G Craig, 'Race', Social Security and Poverty' in J Ditch (ed), *Introduction to Social Security: policies, benefits and poverty*, Routledge, 1999

Seven

Conclusion: the impact and potential of policy intervention

In this chapter consideration is given to the main points that invite policy response from the discussion in the previous chapters. The appropriateness and effectiveness of legislation and policy in these areas is identified, as are the gaps which remain. These points are raised under the broad headings of employment, education, social security and neighbourhood, highlighting first the principal issues and then the responses. First, however, these points are set in the broader context of the limits and possibilities of policy by returning to the issues raised in Chapter 1 concerning the extent to which poverty and deprivation have created and are maintaining a 'divided society'. To what extent are structural and persistent inequalities shaping the fabric of everyday life? What are the implications of poverty and disadvantage and, in particular, the differential disadvantage associated with ethnic group? Is remedial action possible? And if so, what form should it take? Or do policies aimed specifically at disadvantaged groups simply exacerbate their disadvantage? These are obviously large questions and ones to which there are no easy answers. Nevertheless, it is important, I believe, to reflect on them in any evaluation of policies.

In his report in the wake of the Brixton riots of 1981, Lord Scarman identified what might be seen as a social justice agenda as being crucial to the development of a more harmonious society and to repairing and maintaining the 'social fabric'. He went so far as to espouse the use of positive discrimination, seeing in particularised treatment the only sure way of speedily adjusting the disadvantage that was experienced by some groups:

> 'The attack on racial disadvantage must be more direct than it has been. It must be co-ordinated by central government, who with local authorities must ensure that the funds made available are directed to specific areas of racial disadvantage. I have in mind particularly education and employment.

of such documents, as well as projects such as the Performance and Innovation Unit's exploration of *Ethnic Minorities and the Labour Market*, which emanates from the Cabinet Office, suggest that there is a certain momentum behind concern with minority group disadvantage. That such momentum can be mobilised, sustained and prove effective is to be aimed for.

Employment

Unemployment

Chapter 3 identified high rates of unemployment among Pakistanis and Bangladeshis and among young Caribbean men as being a major factor in their excess poverty. Minority groups are also at risk of longer durations of unemployment and poverty. The New Deals are relevant to the young and the long-term unemployed, as well as to lone parents. These have also been subject to evaluation from their initiation and as part of that have collected ethnic group information from participants. While the New Deal for Young People appears to be gaining some success, as Chapter 5 illustrated, the trajectories followed by members of the different minority ethnic groups through and out of it vary. Different patterns can also be seen when the New Deal for the Long-term Unemployed aged 25+ is considered. The results continue to emphasise highly different trajectories for different groups, where structural and cultural factors would *appear* to be interlinked. While Indians are more likely than other groups to move into (unsubsidised) employment, other minority groups are less likely to do so, and Bangladeshis are extremely likely to take up the voluntary sector option. This suggests that the benefit may be least where the disadvantage is greatest. These differences in trajectory may also result from unequal positions among the participants in the scheme. While an obvious difference is educational level, it was, however, those who were most highly qualified who were more likely to move into further training and education options.[6] Education, or attachment to education, may therefore bring with it a different perspective on the labour market as the most appropriate response to disadvantage and discrimination. If this is the case, the New Deal may only be able to be fully effective if and when the wider context of disadvantage is diminished or ameliorated.

The monitoring of outcomes from the New Deals has enabled some perception of their differential impact to be obtained, which in turn has resulted in an attempt to focus on improvements.[7] How successful this can be is not clear. In its recommendations the *Parekh Report* highlighted the adviser role as crucial to the process, implying that it is at that point that the difference is made.[8] However, the Cabinet Office Performance and Innovation Unit, while acknowledging the seriousness of the difference in the otherwise promising New Deal for Young People, emphasised the role of structural factors, such as living in an area of high deprivation, as well as the variation in referral success rates between local offices.[9]

For young people at risk of marginalisation, and for young minority ethnic group members in particular, the ConneXions service was established to aid them in their 'transitional' period (age 13 to 19), with the intention that appropriate intervention could avert those at risk from going on to become part of the young unemployed. However, a study by Britton and others has cast doubt on the ability of the ConneXions service both to identify and maintain contact with their intended constituency, suggesting that there may be a substantial number of unknown young people not in education, employment or training who are not receiving an appropriate response.[10]

Economic inactivity

From the evidence presented in Chapters 3 and 4 there are a number of reasons for below-average rates of economic activity among the different groups. Extended participation in, or return to, education is an issue which is likely to affect Caribbeans in particular. To the extent that this is a consequence of failures within the school system, appropriate approaches in educational policy may offer an answer. For Caribbean women, where early parenthood followed by return to education is a possible explanation, the relevance of educational policy is less clear-cut; though it would still seem to be the case that lone parenthood itself is linked to qualifications levels and educational achievement.[11] While staying on in education accounts in part for the low rates of economic activity among Pakistanis and Bangladeshis, a large amount is explained by very low activity rates among wives and mothers. Cultural patterns, education and employment prospects are intertwined in this phenomenon: female inactivity is strongly related to educational level, and fluency in English is also implicated. However, there may also be a cultural component to these women's qualifications and fluency in English. As Pakistani and Bangladeshi girls improve their educational level – and they now seem to be following the pattern of other girls in outstripping the achievement of boys from their own ethnic group – we might expect to see this pattern decline, but only in so far as educational provision and opportunities for more deprived groups as a whole, and for young Bangladeshi women in particular, are improved. The final reason that has been suggested for low economic activity rates is detachment from the labour market, in so far as restricted and low-paid employment opportunities may not make it viable for one household member to work if the other is unable to. This may be a particular issue where there is a large family to support. Work insertion programmes are unlikely to be of great benefit here, except in so far as they are combined with measures to make work pay. Such measures may be deemed to have potentially the most impact on this latter cause of economic inactivity; and in so far as women suffer from lower pay than men they may impact especially on female economic activity rates.

Making work pay

Somewhat belated recognition of the problem of low pay, particularly in the context of increasing average earnings, has resulted in the introduction of a minimum wage in Britain in 1999. Originally set at £3.60 an hour in April 1999 and subsequently raised to £3.70 and then, in October 2001, to £4.10. It was increased to £4.20 in October 2002. The minimum wage was anticipated to improve the earnings of around two million workers.[12] It was estimated that more than one in ten minority ethnic group workers overall would benefit from the minimum wage, slightly more than the overall proportion of workers anticipated to benefit. In terms of ameliorating minority group poverty this could potentially be seen as a positive initiative. Its impact on particular types of worker could address specific poverty issues among certain minority groups. For example, the increase in wages in restaurant and hotel work, or, possibly, in piece work could be particularly beneficial for minority group members. On the other hand, the bulk of the impact – which was anticipated to be experienced by part-time women workers – would not have such a bearing on those women who are economically inactive (for example, a large proportion of Pakistani and Bangladeshi women) or those working full time (a large proportion of Caribbean women).

As we saw in Chapter 5, while women from black groups have high rates of participation in employment, Pakistani and Bangladeshi women have very low participation rates. But while less than 60 per cent of all women in employment or self-employment work full time, over 70 per cent of women from each of the minority groups who are working work full time, even if the actual rates of participation vary widely between groups.[13] This suggests that the minimum wage might have less impact on such women. On the other hand, the minimum wage was also anticipated to improve the earnings of a fifth of lone parents in employment. Given the high rates of lone parenthood among Caribbean women and the much higher participation rates among Caribbean than among other lone parents, this may be a group that receives particular benefit from the minimum wage, especially when combined with the working families' tax credit.

For those women who are currently economically inactive, the minimum wage may increase the feasibility of employment. On the other hand, the minimum wage on its own does not create employment and if the worklessness of one adult is associated with the worklessness of other adults in the household, then it may prompt little change in inactivity rates.[14] Furthermore, there are issues of enforcement, with anxiety from the Low Pay Commission that minority groups experience worse compliance from employers.[15] On the other hand, to the extent that certain minority groups were concentrated in work paying below the minimum wage in 1998, they are likely to have benefited disproportionately where it has been enforced. This is not to say that the rate is sufficiently high, however. It clearly does not constitute a 'family wage' and thus will not on its own enable those families with a single earner who are paid the minimum to subsist independently.

It was also argued by the Low Pay Commission that one fifth of working 18–20-year-olds would benefit from the development rate of the minimum wage. It is unclear to what extent this will have a positive effect on minority groups. As Chapter 3 showed, a high proportion of this age range from all groups are in education. At the same time, those, such as black Caribbean young men, who are experiencing excess *un*employment cannot expect to benefit either. In addition, despite the recommendations of the Low Pay Commission, the development rate applies to 18–21-year-olds, not to 18–20-year-olds. There is an argument, therefore, that 21-year-olds, who were apparently perceived no differently to other adults by employers, may be penalised relative to other workers by the development rate, which at October 2002 stood at £3.60 an hour. Whether certain ethnic groups are likely to receive a greater impact from the development rate applying to 21-year-olds is not evident. However, the

very fact of differentiation in a standard rate raises the possibility for differential benefit and disadvantage, and therefore for heightening the divisions
within society.

Overall, then, strategies to improve the employment prospects of
those in unemployment or on low pay are likely to be of benefit to minority ethnic groups. To the extent that such strategies are monitored, we are
able, also, to assess them and their impact appropriately. Nevertheless, it
remains clear from the New Deal figures that outcomes from the same
programme may differ across ethnic groups. Including, then, an element
to which such wider programmes are focused or incorporate equality targets could also be seen as beneficial.

Employer discrimination

Despite the existence since 1976 of legislation outlawing discrimination,
direct and indirect, in employment, there is continuing evidence that it persists. It is perhaps the most intractable issue to solve. And evidence such
as that cited on unemployment among young Caribbean men suggests
that the labour market may be becoming more hostile towards some
minorities, even as traditional sectors of employment for certain groups, in
for example manufacturing, break down or disappear.

The 2000 Race Relations Amendment Act saw the first attempt
directly to strengthen the 1976 Act. While it deals largely with public bodies, as discussed below, it also strengthens the power of the Commission
for Racial Equality, which is the most important aspect for an assault on
employer discrimination. Nevertheless, it did not go as far as the
Commission for Racial Equality had proposed in instilling positive duties
on private employers to demonstrate that they are not discriminating.

It has been noted that employers lack incentives to good practice in
equality issues; and the *Parekh Report* identifies required employment
equity plans as the way forward.[16] However, such plans would themselves
require a system of effective monitoring to ensure that they were both
completed and did not become merely paper exercises, but demonstrated a thorough-going commitment. An approach based on encourage-
ment was taken up by the Department for Education and Employment in
1999, when it published guidance for employers which stressed how a
diverse workforce is good for business. However, despite the enthusiastic
endorsement of the Neighbourhood Renewal Unit's Policy Action Team on
jobs, it is clear that such initiatives can only form part of an approach to

transforming the employment context.[17] The Policy Action Team itself accompanies the recommendation of this strategy with recommendations for practical help to business, including in the area of monitoring, and incorporating equality measures into standards for business. Again, such measures may not fully resolve the issue of employer discrimination, but messages sent out through making equality part of an overall employment agenda are the way of ensuring that equality and discrimination are regarded seriously.

Education

Skills deficits

As has been identified, poverty among minority ethnic groups can in part be traced to the decline of traditional sectors of employment and the lack of appropriate skills for meeting the demands of a high-skill and service-based economy. While minority group members have been relatively successful in making the transition following industrialisation,[18] this relative success does not mean absolutely good prospects. In fact, the evidence on young Caribbean men suggests that their current prospects are particularly bleak. Emphasis has, therefore, been placed on appropriate education and training that will fit young people to the jobs that are now available and will compensate for past social class and minority group-related labour market disadvantage. While there has been much talk of equality of opportunity and the creation of a meritocracy, it is not clear that educational policy has been particularly successful in creating such opportunities, or whether the approaches favoured are the most appropriate ones.

Following the major changes which occurred to educational provision in the late 1980s with the reduction of local education authority control, increased parental and governor control and opportunities for schools to 'opt out' into grant maintained status, a fragmentation of the education system and increasing polarisation between 'good' and 'bad' schools has been observed. This polarisation has heightened the disadvantage experienced by those who cannot obtain access to the preferred schools. The Labour Government ended the opt-out into grant maintained status, and has pursued a policy of substantial investment in schooling. However, as we have seen, while overall achievement continues to rise, the gap between achievers and non-achievers also continues to grow. To what extent is this issue being effectively dealt with?

The Department for Education and Skills' recent education White Paper, *Schools Achieving Success*, explicitly acknowledges that gaps in achievement associated with neighbourhood, with social class and with ethnic group are a blight on the school system. Yet it does not seem clear that the proposals in the paper will ensure that the gap is closed rather than widened and, specifically, whether the proposals will contribute to greater attainment among those minority ethnic groups which are faring less well in school. The paper combines messages of increased individuality with increased inspection and monitoring. Options for diversification and additional funding are highlighted with the continued promotion of 'beacon schools', with support for faith schools, and with the promotion of specialist schools able to select pupils in the (limited) subjects in which they choose to specialise. While there has been anxiety in some quarters about the potentially divisive nature of all faith schools, others see them as vehicles for improving standards among the religious groups catered for. In the case of Muslims this could lead to a reduction in educational inequality. What is perhaps more germane is the prospective composition of schools. The evidence suggests that, despite some individual school variation, it is the overall social class composition of pupils that is critical to levels of achievement within school. Thus a pupil in a school of predominantly middle class children is likely to fare better than they would in a school of predominantly working class children. There would seem to be the danger in such proposals as those for special schools that the emphasis on diversity is liable to lead to hierarchy. The history of education in this country has shown that 'different but equal' is not a position which is sustainable. The promotion of diversity and the increasing options to bid for central funds for particular status or programmes for particular schools seems hardly likely to decrease gaps in educational achievement, especially in so far as such gaps are related, at least in part, to social class background. It may well be that specialist schools perform well in comparison to other schools, but it seems somewhat contradictory to both assert their relatively strong performance and suggest that they will not widen differential attainment rates between schools. If specialist schools are good for their pupils then the obvious corollary is that non-specialist schools are less good. A simple refutation, as given in the White Paper, does not seem sufficient response to this concern: 'There are those who have said that specialist schools will create a two tier system. They won't.'[19]

A recent initiative developed especially in relation to the issue of achievement within minority ethnic groups is the Ethnic Minority Achievement Grant, established in 1998. Local education authorities can put in detailed bids for central government funds to support projects that are designed to improve the achievement of certain minority groups. There is a similar programme for traveller children. 1n 1999, 12 local education authorities submitted bids for different programmes; in 2000/01 the funds available under this grant were over £160 million. It has replaced the funding that used to be available under Section 11 of the Local Government Act 1966. While it is intended to and may well encourage interesting and innovative schemes, again the focus on special applications for special programmes may not be the most appropriate way of systematically improving achievement.[20] As the discussion of area issues suggests, the expectation of finding solutions to structural problems in individual and individually supported initiatives may well be misplaced. And from the perspective of the Cantle Report, they can even be counter-productive. Furthermore, Gillborn and Mirza identified the way that the statistics used to support applications for the grant were often of poor quality and poorly used.[21] This returns to the issue of ethnic monitoring and the way that, despite it having been operated in schools for some years, it is often not carried with sufficient commitment or skill either to provide appropriate information or to enable the development of policy.

Attempts to increase staying on at school, particularly from those working class children whose post-compulsory participation has tended to be lower, has led to the piloting of education maintenance allowances. These allowances amount to a training grant, which is supplied direct to children from low-income families who stay on in post-16 education up to the age of 18. Evaluation of these pilots would appear to be positive, and they will be adopted nationally in 2004. Given the patterns of staying on in education that are greatest among Indians and Chinese but also higher than average at age 18 among other minority ethnic groups, and given their greater probability of being in a low-income family, it seems likely that education maintenance allowances would particularly benefit these groups. On the other hand, if children from minority groups are going to stay on in school anyway, it diminishes the incentive effect of the allowance, though it may increase the welfare of the children while they continue in school. Nevertheless, the possibility of support for years during which minority groups are effectively compensating for disadvantage past or prospective seems potentially a positive step. Again, it is a proposal that may disproportionately affect minority group members without being specifically targeted on them. This highlights the way in which social class-based initiatives can have a positive impact on minority groups' experience.

Exclusions, labelling, within-school racism

Chapter 5 also drew attention to the ways in which within-school factors could result in under-achievement over the school life of a child. One of the issues that had been highlighted was the high level of exclusions experienced by Caribbeans, and Caribbean boys in particular. Explanations suggested that cross-cultural misunderstandings and labelling of pupils had been major causal factors. In addition, the potential for responses to pupils to create 'self-fulfilling prophecies' has been attested. The extensive attention that was given to the issue of differential rates of exclusion has resulted in a substantial reduction in the rates among Caribbean pupils, but they still remain disproportionately high, affecting as many as 0.5 per cent of Caribbean schoolchildren. The recognition of this issue through monitoring, with the consequent development of strategies for dealing with it, which could themselves be monitored, highlights the issue of effective monitoring as one important tool in combating the perpetuation of within-school disadvantage. However, the Government has since abandoned its targets on reducing school exclusions, and they have subsequently risen again.

Monitoring is one of the four key elements that the Department for Education and employment identified in its proposals in 2000, *Removing the Barriers: raising achievement levels for minority ethnic pupils*. The other three areas that were identified as crucial at the within-school level were high expectations of achievement, the culture and ethos of the school, and parental involvement. While the issue of expectations focuses on teachers and their attitudes and responses to pupils, the issue of culture and school ethos raises the issues of relations between pupils. The extent to which schools can foster division or harmony is an issue that was also raised by Macpherson in his report of inquiry into the death of Stephen Lawrence. The report contained a number of recommendations concerning education and the curriculum as a result of which citizenship studies will be required in order to develop understandings of Britain as a multi-cultural society. The *Parekh Report* further stressed the role of inspection as a means for ascertaining and requiring a race equality and diversity dimension to school practice.[22] The question remains, of course, as to whether children learn values at home or at school, and also how they learn them.

Social security

Out-of-work benefits

The principal out-of-work benefits are income support and jobseeker's allowance, which have the same rates. For those of pension age there is the minimum income guarantee, which also has its origins in income support. For those out of work, the crucial issue is whether benefits provide sufficiently to support those reliant on them. From the Government's perspective, the pressures to provide adequate support are balanced against overall expenditure on the benefits and potential disincentives to take up paid employment if benefits are adequate. Income support and its predecessors have not matched up to calculations of minimum needs. That is still the case and as certain minority groups are more dependent on income support, so they will in aggregate suffer more from its inadequacy. However, in recent years there have been some substantial increases in the levels of certain aspects of the benefits. The minimum income guarantee, while not lavish, has been increased above the rates provided by the previous pensioner premiums. The irrelevance of work incentive concerns for the older population has been one means to its increase. As discussed, minority ethnic groups have been less likely to build up assets or gain occupational pensions. The rates of means-tested support in old age are therefore particularly relevant to them. A substantial increase has also, as Table 2.2 illustrated, been made to the allowance of younger children, equalising the amount allowed for all children under 16. This is likely to have a disproportionate effect on the poorest minority groups – Bangladeshis and Pakistanis – who tend to have larger families and where claimants are more likely to have young children. While then, income support cannot be seen as a positive option for any ethnic groups, these recent changes have at least not had a negative effect on minority group members. On the other hand, the removal of the lone-parent premium for new claimants, which took place in 1997, to widespread backbench and poverty lobby outrage,[23] is likely to have impacted disproportionately on Caribbean group, given the relatively high rates of lone parenthood within that group.

In-work benefits

The working families' tax credit, which was introduced in October 1999, replacing family credit, has been designed to raise incomes across all those with families, and similarly the disabled person's tax credit has been substituted for the staggeringly unsuccessful disability working allowance. These credits are designed to increase the income of those working but with extra costs (children or a disability) that might make earnings insufficient to remain out of poverty. Further, the child tax credit acknowledges the extra costs of children for all families except those in the top tax bracket. The working tax credit will, from April 2003, extend tax credit support to those without children and in full-time work. It will be dependent on income and will incorporate the disabled person's tax credit, the 50+ unemployment credit and the adult component of working families' tax credit. The introduction of the minimum wage prior to the introduction of working families' tax credit means that the credit does not simply subsidise low pay. Instead, given that beyond a certain applicable amount the benefit is only withdrawn at a proportion of the gain in income (55 per cent), the possibility for increasing income through longer hours and higher earnings while yet remaining on the benefit is enhanced.[24] In addition, the benefit has an increased element payable to those who work more than 30 hours a week, and there is also the option for those on the benefit to claim 70 per cent of childcare costs up to a maximum level. As has been mentioned, information on benefit claims is not available by ethnic group. However, the *Family Resources Survey* indicates that black, Indian and Pakistani and Bangladeshi benefit families all make proportionately greater use of working families' tax credit than families overall: a finding that is hardly surprising given the higher proportions of families with dependent children within this group. On the other hand, there may be greater problems with take-up among minority ethnic groups, as discussed in Chapter 6, and accessing appropriate and affordable childcare to enable use of both the benefit and the childcare element may be particularly difficult for those in deprived areas.[25] The Government has acknowledged the issue of childcare in deprived areas in its National Childcare Strategy, and both the commitments there and the operation of the Sure Start programme in deprived areas may alleviate some of the difficulty. More information will be obtained with the ongoing evaluation of Sure Start.

Given the prevalence of Caribbean lone parents, and their increased likelihood of working and of working full time, the increased generosity of working families' tax credit compared to family credit may be particularly advantageous for this group. Problems of interaction between working families' tax credit and housing benefit may continue, but on the other hand, the increment for working over 30 hours and the childcare allowances may benefit this group. The small number of Bangladeshi and Pakistani *lone* parents is least likely to be able to benefit from working families' tax credit.[26] However, for couple-parent families, especially where there are large numbers of children, the working families' tax credit may offer opportunities to escape the high rates of severe in-work poverty that were identified by Berthoud. One caution is the difficulty, noted in the last chapter, of claiming in-work benefits when self-employed. Insofar as working families' tax credit subsidises low pay, however, it is not a solution to labour market disadvantage or the operation of discriminatory practices in relation to members of minority ethnic groups.

As with the minimum wage, working families' tax credit may have some potential for reducing inactivity rates. But that depends critically on employment opportunities being available, on the willingness of employers to take on the administration associated with the benefit, and on a relative absence of employer discrimination.

From 2003, both working families' tax credit and the child elements of income support /Income-based jobseeker's allowance will be incorporated into the integrated child credit. An expansion of the credit system that enables the credit to be paid to both those in work and those not in work, the integrated child credit is part of the Chancellor of the Exchequer's project to provide a more adequate basis of support for families with children. The Child Poverty Action Group, however, while welcoming any transfer of resources towards children would prefer a system based on increasing the rates of the universal child benefit;[27] a recommendation also made in the *Parekh Report*. Which of these two routes would more surely be positive for minority ethnic groups is hard to assess. However, it is clear that any system which tends to redistribute funds towards families with children is likely to have a relatively beneficial effect on the poorest of the minority groups, Pakistanis and Bangladeshis. That is, of course, if take-up and delivery are not an issue.

Take-up

There is a need for understanding more clearly patterns of eligible non-claiming to ensure that issues of take-up are addressed. While it is not an issue specifically addressed in the Department for Work and Pension's race equality consultation document, there is a stress there on effective communication, both through publications in appropriate languages and through outreach work.[28] Thus, information obstacles are being acknowledged and addressed. In addition, its responsibilities under the Race Relations Amendment Act 2000 clearly indicate the need for ethnic monitoring of claimants – a step which would dramatically enhance the understanding of minority groups' receipt of benefit and their experience of the service. However, the timescale and plans for the introduction of ethnic monitoring reveal an understandable caution about the demands of the task. Other aspects of delivery that may have an impact on the take-up of benefits, such as the manner of treatment, *should* also come within the scope of the requirements of the Race Relations Amendment Act and the Department's proposals for monitoring satisfaction and differential impact. However, reluctance to claim based on the stigma of means-tested benefits themselves will only be reduced by a lesser call on such benefits, that is, a reduction in labour market and other forms of disadvantage.

Area issues

Neighbourhood deprivation

Given the geographical concentration of ethnic minorities discussed in Chapters 2 and 5, it might be thought that schemes targeted towards peculiarly deprived areas would be of particular relevance to the different minority groups.

Area-based initiatives have a long history. They go back at least as far as the Educational Priority Areas of the late 1960s and they are sometimes traced to the public health and clearance programmes of the nineteenth century.[29] The period of Conservative government from 1979 to 1997, saw a plethora of re-inventions and repackaging of an urban programme,[30] culminating in the amalgamation of the schemes into the Single Regeneration Budget in the early 1990s. Despite little demonstrable improvement in areas of urban decay over the quarter century up to 1994,[31] the Labour Government has shown as great a zeal for locality-based schemes since 1997 as its predecessors. The stress on social inclusion adopts an understanding of exclusion as a phenomenon which can affect an area as well as an individual, and initiatives which can demonstrate cross-departmental working, or 'joined-up' thinking and local involvement have been extensively promoted as one of the principal solutions to deprived areas. We thus have, alongside the Single Regeneration Budget, Education, Health and Employment Action Zones, as well as the New Deal for Communities and a National Strategy for Neighbourhood Renewal, which comes under the direction of the Neighbourhood Renewal Unit in the Office of the Deputy Prime Minister. It might be anticipated that such a level of activity would create a positive impact in deprived areas and thus have a beneficial effect on those minority groups who are especially deprived and especially concentrated in deprived areas.

However, a number of problems remain with this approach. First is the ecological fallacy: the fact that there are more poor people living in non-deprived areas than in deprived areas, and many of the people in deprived areas will not in fact be poor. This relates to the issue of where resources go. Resources for deprived areas do not necessarily benefit the poorest in those areas, and in particular there is evidence that minority ethnic groups have gained less from targeted neighbourhood funds than their presence warrants.[32] At the same time, the perception of targeted resources and their ('undeserving') recipients in a context of scarce resources can create tension and heighten incipient resentments and divisions, as Cantle's report demonstrated. Furthermore there is the danger that cosmetic measures that improve specific aspects of an area or its appearance, or, similarly, processes of gentrification will not necessarily benefit the original residents – or may shift them and their problems elsewhere. People who are resident in deprived areas are predominantly constrained by their lack of options for housing mobility; measures for mitigation of area disadvantage therefore have to dovetail with housing policy. But it is hard to see how current housing policy, which is both somewhat sketchy and emphasises notions of choice, can work effectively for those for whom 'choices' are severely constrained.[33] Finally, as Philo has pointed out, the problems of and solutions for deprived neighbourhoods cannot necessarily be found within the areas themselves:

> 'The roots of poverty are *not* straightforwardly to be found within the places and regions affected (somehow neatly sealed within their geographical boundaries). Rather, the causes of poverty 'in place' derive from many different sources and locations beyond that place, and this must be taken on board in policy formulation and execution.'[34]

If this point is not recognised, there is the danger that a focus on particular deprived areas will simply serve to problematise them, and thus their residents, further. This could be a particular issue as the problems of deprivation of an area become associated with particular minority groups. Greater understanding of the impact of the most recent locally-based schemes and their impact on minority ethnic groups' experience will become available following the evaluation of the New Deal for Communities.

Public services

The Macpherson inquiry into the handling of the murder of Stephen Lawrence highlighted the extent of 'institutional racism' that existed within the Metropolitan Police,[35] and prompted new race relations legislation, which would enshrine in law expectations on public bodies for clearly demonstrating that their practices were non-discriminatory. The Race Relations Amendment Act 2000 provides for a duty on public bodies (and private bodies performing public functions, such as private security forces working in prisons) not to discriminate in carrying out *any* of their functions. It also creates a positive duty on public authorities (a more limited group than public bodies covered above) to demonstrate that they are taking consideration of issues of racial equality in their activities. It also strengthens the power of the Commission for Racial Equality, enabling it to enforce compliance with its recommendations through the courts if necessary. The expectation is that local authorities and other public authorities will take far more positive action to combat discrimination, including more effective monitoring to be able to demonstrate such activity and its success. With what energy public authorities approach this responsibility and what the impact will be, remains to be seen.

Conclusions: what direction for an anti-poverty policy for minority ethnic groups?

So what are the main directions that policy would do well to pursue if the excess poverty of particular minority groups is to be ameliorated? Here a number of recurrent issues are briefly highlighted, which are essential to the fuller understanding of the causes and processes of ethnic minority groups' poverty and for its effective amelioration.

The first issue is that of ethnic monitoring. The collection of comprehensive information, at as disaggregated a level as possible, on the ethnicity of employees and users of services and public and private provision can only enhance our understanding of the extent of minority group disadvantage, the differences between groups and the possible causes or associated factors. There is now broad recognition of the need for ethnic monitoring and its importance from within government and from campaigners, as well as from the Commission for Racial Equality. Yet that recognition has not been translated into comprehensive action. In addition, the issues of sensitivity to resistance regarding the collection of such information and the appropriateness of different classifications with different types and degrees of differentiation for different contexts need to be more widely understood. Only then will both sufficient and meaningful information become available to policy makers and academics alike to enable a less tentative conclusion about the process by which a particular ethnicity relates to a greater risk of poverty.

The second issue is that of effective legislation and its enforcement. The Race Relations Amendment Act has placed the onus on public authorities to demonstrate that they are complying with the requirements of race relations legislation. It has also given the Commission for Racial Equality greater power to enforce this duty. The effects of direct and indirect discrimination, which can lead to or exacerbate minority groups' disadvantage, require an opportunity for effective redress. It remains to be seen how the recent legislation performs in terms of creating more equal opportunities for those from different groups.

The poverty of minority groups is partly a function of the inequalities and rates of poverty within society as a whole. Their heightened disadvantage would be less problematic if the social structure did not enable the existence of extreme inequalities and the existence of a substantial group of people in poverty. Thus, measures which reduce inequalities within society as a whole are likely to mitigate the disadvantage of minority groups, and to be relatively advantageous to the more deprived groups. Highlighted in the discussion of benefits, the minimum wage, and education is how those measures which tend to be broadly equalising are likely to benefit minority groups and may lead to a reduction in their disadvantaged position over time. To such measures might be added a more progressive taxation system, or even a basic income scheme.[36]

The final issue is the necessity for an ongoing recognition of diversity of experience both within and between groups. While I have shown a certain scepticism towards explanations of poverty that draw on assumptions about the 'cultural' characteristics of different minority groups, at the same time it is important not to homogenise the experience of those who do engage in practices, or lifestyles, or make choices that differ significantly from those of the population as a whole. Such different experiences can be related to excess poverty, for example, through the greater prevalence of lone parents or large families among Caribbeans and Bangladeshis respectively. Accounting for such poverty simply in structural terms raises two dangers. First, that the excess poverty will, by those means, be discounted. Second, that we fail to investigate or question why it is that certain practices or choices are penalised relative to others. Continuing to explore the diversity of experience within and between groups and its relationship to greater or lesser degrees of poverty and disadvantage enables us not only to understand some of the factors contributing to that poverty, but also to interrogate some of the assumptions on which the policy process itself is built.

Notes

1 Lord Scarman, *The Scarman Report: the Brixton disorders 10-12 April 1981*, Penguin, 1982, p210

2 T Cantle (chair), *Community Cohesion: a report of the independent review team chaired by Ted Cantle*, Home Office, December 2001, p9

3 See note 2, p10

4 This is despite the fact that it was pointed out at the time of the riots that it was a middle class exodus from the areas where the riots occurred rather than a specifically white exodus that had exacerbated the problems suffered by those living there.

5 M Young, *The Rise of the Meritocracy, 1870-2033: an essay on education and equality*, Thames and Hudson, 1958

6 Department for Work and Pensions, 'New Deal for Young People and Long-term Unemployed People aged 25+: Statistics to December 2001', *Statistics First Release*, February 2002

7 See Performance and Innovation Unit, *Ethnic Minorities and the Labour Market: interim analytical report*, Cabinet Office, 2001, p134

8 B Parekh, *The Future of Multi-ethnic Britain,* (The Parekh Report), Profile Books, 2000, p308

9 See note 7

10 L Britton, B Chatrik, B Coles, G Craig, C Hylton, and S Mumtaz, *Missing ConneXions: the career dynamics and welfare needs of black and minority ethnic young people at the margins*, The Policy Press, 2002

11 R Berthoud, 'Family Formation in Multi-cultural Britain: three patterns of diversity', Paper 2000-34, *Working Papers of the Institute for Social and Economic Research*, University of Essex, December 2000, p9

12 Low Pay Commission, *The National Minimum Wage, First Report*, Cm3976, June 1998, p5

13 Department of Social Security, *Family Resources Survey Great Britain 1999-2000*, 2001, Table 2.6, p18

14 P Gregg and J Wadsworth, 'More Work in Fewer Households?' in J Hills, *New Inequalities: the changing distribution of income and wealth in the United Kingdom*, CUP, 1996

15 See note 7, p137

16 See note 8, p307

17 Policy Action Team on jobs (PAT1), *Jobs for All: national strategy for neighbourhood renewal*, DfEE, 1999

18 P Iganski and G Payne, 'Socio-economic Restructuring and Employment: the case of minority ethnic groups', *The British Journal of Sociology*, 50, 1999

19 Department for Education and Skills, *Schools Achieving Success*, 2001, p40

20 *The Parekh Report* suggested that the grant should specifically fund schemes which tackled issues of exclusions from school and that schemes funded should be independently evaluated (see note 8, p300).

21 D Gillborn and H Mirza, *Educational Inequality: mapping race, class and gender*, Ofsted, 2000, p11

22 See note 8, p301

23 See J Bradshaw, 'Child Poverty under Labour' in G Fimister (ed), *An End in Sight? Tackling child poverty in the UK*, CPAG, 2001

24 This taper of 55 per cent and a higher applicable amount as the starting point at which benefit is reduced make this a more generous benefit than its predecessor, family credit, and therefore also liable to benefit families with children across a much wider range of the income distribution.

25 See note 7

26 L Platt and M Noble, *'Race', Place and Poverty*, Joseph Rowntree Foundation, 1999, p34

27 M Barnes and G Fimister, 'Children's Benefits and Credits: is an integrated child credit the answer?' in G Fimister (ed), *An End in Sight? Tackling child poverty in the UK*, CPAG, 2001

28 Department for Work and Pensions, *Equality, Opportunity and Independence for All*, Race Equality Scheme: Consultation, 2002

29 See for example, M Goodwin, 'Poverty in the City' in C Philo (ed), *Off the Map: the social geography of poverty in the UK*, CPAG, 1995

30 B Robson, *Those Inner Cities*, Clarendon, 1988

31 T Bovaird, 'Managing Urban Economic Development: learning to change or the marketing of failure?', *Urban Studies* 31, 1994

32 S J Smith, *The Politics of 'Race' and Residence*, Polity, 1989

33 Department of Environment, Transport and the Regions (now Office of the Deputy Prime Minister), *Quality and Choice: a decent home for all*, 2000

34 C Philo, *Off the Map: the social geography of poverty in the UK*, CPAG, 1995

35 Sir W Macpherson, *The Stephen Lawrence Inquiry: report of an inquiry*, The Stationery Office, 1999

36 See B Jordan, *A Theory of Poverty and Social Exclusion*, Polity, 1996, for advocacy of a basic income scheme.

Appendix one
Further reading

There are a number of topics which are critical to the experience of minority group members that are not explicitly covered within the scope of this book, the principal two being health and housing. While poverty has implications for health and while housing and residence are bound up with socio-economic status, there is not room within this volume to do justice to the wealth of research in these two areas. Some discussion of housing is necessary in the discussions of area effects and settlement patterns, but it is not treated as a distinct topic. For readers who are interested in discussion of minority groups' experiences in these two areas, particularly in relation to poverty and socio-economic status and poverty the following sources are recommended:

Health

Department of Health, *Independent Inquiry into Inequalities in Health* (The Acheson Report), The Stationery Office, 1997

This provides a synthesis on evidence of and research into health inequalities. It covers social class and income inequalities but also inequalities experienced by particular groups including ethnic minorities.

J Y Nazroo, *The Health of Britain's Ethnic Minorities: findings from a national survey*, Policy Studies Institute, 1997

This is analysis of the health information collected by the 1993 *Fourth National Survey of Ethnic Minorities*. It also provides a useful discussion of different frameworks for investigating and explaining observed health differences between ethnic groups.

Further sources for ethnic minorities and health inequalities include:
W I U Ahmad, *'Race' and Health in Contemporary Britain*, Open University Press, 1993
R Balarajan, 'Ethnicity and Variations in the Nation's Health', *Health Trends* 27, 1995, pp114-119

R Balarajan and V Soni Raleigh, *Ethnicity and Health in England*, HMSO, 1995

H Cooper, C S Smaje and S L Arber, 'Use of Health Services by Children and Young People According to Ethnicity and Social Class: secondary analysis of a national survey', *British Medical Journal* 317, 1998, pp1047-1051

H Cooper, C S Smaje and S L Arber, 'Equity in Health Service Use by Children: examining the ethnic paradox', *Journal of Social Policy* 28, 1999, pp457-478

J Y Nazroo, *Ethnicity, Class and Health*, Policy Studies Institute, 2001

C Smaje, Health, *'Race', and Ethnicity: making sense of the evidence*, King's Fund, 1995

C Smaje and J Le Grand, 'Ethnicity, Equity and the Use of Health Services in the British National Health Service', *Social Science and Medicine* 45, 1997, pp485-96

Housing

R Tomlins, *Housing Experiences of Minority Ethnic Communities in Britain: an academic literature review and annotated bibliography*, Centre for Research in Ethnic Relations, University of Warwick, 1999

This provides both a short overview of the housing experiences of minority ethnic groups and details of the major publications in the field of minority groups and housing from the early 1960s to the late 1990s.

V Karn, *Ethnicity in the 1991 Census: Volume four: employment, education and housing among the ethnic minority populations of Britain*, The Stationery Office, 1997

This edited volume provides detailed analysis from the Census in relation to a number of aspects of housing experience.

H Green *et al*, *Housing In England: a report of the survey of English housing*, HMSO, 2000

This is an annual publication deriving from the *Survey of English Housing* which includes information on minority ethnic groups' experience of housing and trends in their tenure and housing patterns.

Further works including some older, but nevertheless significant, ones are:

J Lakey, 'Neighbourhoods and Housing' in T Modood, R Berthoud *et al*, *Ethnic Minorities in Britain: diversity and disadvantage*, Policy Studies Institute, 1997, pp184-223

P Sarre, D Phillips and R Skellington, *Ethnic Minority Housing: explanations and policies*, Avebury, 1989

S J Smith, *The Politics of 'Race' and Residence: citizenship, segregation and white supremacy in Britain*, Polity, 1989

P Somerville and A Steele, *'Race', Housing and Social Exclusion*, Jessica Kingsley, 2002